Nowell's Middle Catechism

A CATECHISM, OR INSTITUTION OF CHRISTIAN RELIGION,

to be learned of all youth, next after the little Catechism: appointed in
THE BOOK OF COMMON PRAYER

Originally printed at London, by John Day, dwelling over Aldersgate, in the year of Our Lord, 1572.

ANDREW E. BRASHIER, EDITOR

Copyright © 2024

By Andrew England Brashier

Nowell's Middle Catechism is in the public domain. Regarding all other materials contained herein, all other rights reserved, including the right to reproduce this book or portions thereof in any form whatsoever without the expressed consent of the author.

Table of Contents

Editor's Philosophy 4

Editor's Foreword 5

Alexander Nowell, A Life 8

Nowell's Original Foreword 15

CHRISTIAN RELIGION 18

I. The Law: 22

The Ten Commandments......................22

II. The Gospel: 49

The Apostles' Creed 49

III. Praying: 102

The Lord's Prayer................................102

IV. The Holy Sacraments......................124

A Selection of Prayers for Students & Scholars

An admonition for *the morning.* 136

A Psalm for *the morning.* 138

A Prayer for *the morning.*....................140

A Morning Prayer *for scholars.*............142

Another Prayer *for scholars.* 144

An admonition for *the evening and night.* 145

The Psalms for *the evening and night.*..................147

A Prayer for *the evening and night.*......................150

Another Prayer for *evening and night*................152

Editor's Philosophy

My edits consist of changing British spellings into American spellings (i.e. removing "u" from "honour") updating old spellings (i.e. "vertue" is now "virtue"), adding headings, emboldening the questions, and updating the Scriptural and apocryphal abbreviations for easier use. On occasion I added footnotes where I thought clarity was needed. My goal was to allow the text to speak for itself. The Scriptural citations derive from an earlier printing that took some time to "decipher" as the citation system was unique to that particular printing. Any errors in "deciphering" the Scriptural citations are my own.

Editor's Foreword

Many reading this catechism will think yet it is quite long, without properly considering the time in which it was harvested. The need to ensure an accurate articulation of the Gospel impelled and compelled it: Reformation necessitates renewal. Hence and ever since the Reformation the Church must articulate the Gospel in order to remember, preserve, protect, and educate the next generation who are going to take up the mantle and orchestrate the Great Commission. For now, consider this small contribution ever anchored upon our one faith.

The "Middle" Catechism ultimately clocks in shorter than Nowell's Longer Catechism, but is robustly full of the same content. While the simplicity of the shorter classic prayer book catechism is to be commended, one can quickly tell why Nowell expanded his original work in the traditional prayer book and wrote longer catechisms for bringing up children in the faith. The

1604 Canons required[1] schoolmasters to teach their students either "the longer or shorter catechism," which refers to this work.

Nowell's work, unlike other catechisms circulating during the English Reformation, received official recognition and serves as a lens through which contemporary Anglicans may see not only their past, but also their future – if Anglicanism desires to unite under common doctrine and faith. That "if" is a large question and even those provinces pledging fidelity to the Anglican formularies through the Jerusalem Declaration have much work to do by educating their parishes and clergy alike as to what it means to be Anglican and what is the faith we profess.

I pray this republication will serve to benefit many households of faith, parishes, and dioceses across

---

[1] Canon LXXIX.

Anglicanism and beyond – starting with my own beloved family.

Cara, my darling wife I love your devotion to our Lord and our family. Holland, seek wisdom – which is your middle name, *Sophia* – through the Holy Scriptures this catechism points you towards. Beckett, fervently desire, seek, and proclaim what is true and beautiful as only reflected in the divine and holy Word of God. Colman, manfully fight under Christ's banner against sin, the world, and the devil, and continue as Christ's faithful soldier by being equipped with the two edged sword.

In Christ Jesus,
Andrew++
Feast of St. Augustin, Bishop of Hippo
August 29, 2024

Alexander Nowell, A Life

Early Life

Northern England seems to have produced more than its fair share of Reformers during the 1500s. Ridley, Grindal, Coverdale, Sandys, and others all hailed from the northern counties of Lancashire, Yorkshire, Durham, Northumberland, and Westmoreland. Nowell is another one of this group, chiefly remembered today for the three catechisms that he compiled between 1562 and 1572, and for his 42 years as Dean of St Paul's.

Nowell was born at Reed Hall, near Clitheroe, Lancashire somewhere between 1507 and 1517. He first enters the written record as a pupil of Middleton Grammar School, near Manchester, then as a fellow of Brasenose College, Oxford, in 1526 which suggests that he was born 1510-12. It is unknown when and by whom he was ordained, but he was appointed as second Headmaster of Westminster School in 1543, continuing there until he fled into exile in 1553.

Exile and Return

He spent the years of Mary I's reign in Strassburg and then in Frankfurt-am-Main where he became embroiled in the dispute between Richard Coxe, former tutor to Elizabeth I, and John Knox, the future Reformer of Scotland, over the direction of the English congregation. Nowell seems to have been close to Knox, but when he and the other radicals departed for Basle or Geneva, he remained in Frankfurt for the rest of his exile.

Nowell returned to England, along with the bulk of the exiles, in 1559. Shortly after his return he was appointed as domestic chaplain to Edmund Grindal, the new Bishop of London, a fellow northerner who soon made him Archdeacon of Middlesex, then Dean of St. Paul's in 1561. It was as Dean of St.

Paul's that he preached the sermon that opened the 1562/3 session of Convocation at which he served as Prolocutor (Speaker) of the Lower House of Convocation. This Convocation proved to be important in deciding the eventual shape of the English Reformation. Further reforms such as the abolition of organs and professional choirs were proposed and defeated by only one vote. A revised version of the Articles of Religion was debated and approved, and lastly, Nowell's 'Catechism' was approved by Convocation to supplement that in the Prayer Book.

The Catechism

There had always been an awareness that the Prayer Book Catechism, sometimes attributed to Nowell, was inadequate. John Ponet, a close associate of Thomas Cranmer's, had drawn up a 'Short Catechism' in 1551-52 which had widely circulated before the Marian reaction, frequently printed as 'one book' with the Forty-two Articles. This examined the Decalogue, Creed, Sacraments, and Lord's Prayer, and maintained a Reformed and Infralapsarian theology. It reflected the growing influence of Bucer and Bullinger on the English theological scene but was criticized in the eighteenth century as 'Calvinistic.' Overall, it reflected the theological positions of Strassburg and Zurich to the point where Bullinger was particularly enthusiastic about it and circulated it amongst his fellow Reformers.

Ponet's *Small Catechism* also served as one of the source texts for Nowell's Catechism alongside the much better-known Catechism composed by John Calvin in 1558. For all that Nowell's 'Catechism' is something of a scissors and paste job, it does show a certain independence on some points. For example, Predestination is hardly addressed in Nowell's text reflecting its relative low priority in English theology in the early-1560s, and it hedges between the traditional and Calvinist views on the Decent of Christ into Hell. Its teaching on the sacraments is also firmly in the tradition set by Bucer and Cranmer in the late-1540s reflecting the moderate Reformed stance of the English Church. Originally published in Latin, and translated into English in 1572, it exists in Long, Middle, and Short versions, of which the second was the most widely circulated.

For all that Nowell's Catechism is regarded today as the Elizabethan Catechism, it should not be thought that it had sole possession of the field. Recent work by Dr. Anthony Milton of the University of Sheffield has shown that the Heidelberg Catechism, along with the commentaries by its author Ursinus, as well as that by Jeremias Bastingius, had considerable influence in the Church of England in the reigns of Elizabeth I, James I, and Charles I. Calvin's Catechism was used in the universities alongside Nowell's, and the Heidelberg from the 1560s to the 1630s. However, whereas its competitors seem to have been large forgotten after 1660, Nowell's Catechism survived the Interregnum, was reprinted in the reign of Charles II, and was translated into Welsh as late as 1809, suggesting an enduring significance in the life of the Church.

Later Career

After his prominent role in the 1562/3 Convocation, Nowell's career seems to have stalled. An unfortunate sermon before Queen Elizabeth urging her to marry is the cause traditionally ascribed for his lack of further promotion. Instead of proceeding to the bishopric that his talents and connection would have indicated lay in his future, Nowell remained as Dean of St Paul's.

In his private life, Nowell was twice married, but left no children. He was an enthusiastic angler who often donated his catch to the poor, and it was this hobby that led to his other, accidental, boon to humanity – bottled beer. He had taken some beer with him on a bottle to quench his thirst whilst out by the river. At the end of the day, he left without his bottle, rediscovering it a week later, he found it to be "not so much a bottle as a gun" as the secondary fermentation meant that it opened with a resounding 'pop,' and had also much improved the flavour of the beer!

Alexander Nowell lived into a ripe old age, dying February 13th, 1602, at the age of somewhere between 85 and 95. He was buried in the church he had served for so many years, St. Paul's Cathedral.

+PDR Sept. 6th, 2024
The Most Rev. Peter D. Robinson
Presiding Bishop,
United Episcopal Church of North America

To the most Reverend Fathers in God, my Lords,
Mathew Archbishop of Canterbury, Edmond Archbishop of York, Edwin Bishop of London, and the rest of the Bishops in England.

It is not unknown unto your Wisdoms, that the diversity of Catechisms, in shortness or in length, either for the first entering of children or for the more full instruction of youth, in the principles and sum of Christian Religion, are as well allowed by the judgments of diverse godly and learned men, as also practiced of many Christian Churches in sundry Countries well reformed, not without good reason, grounded upon the diversities of Ages, and capacity of Wits. I therefore, upon the said Considerations, have applied myself in this Catechism, being of a *middle* sort, both to further the profit, and to satisfy the minds of such as may judge the *little* Catechism as written for very young Children, not fully enough to serve for their instruction; and on the other part may think the *larger* Catechism[2] to be too long and tedious, either for their capacity or leisure. For their use (I say) and satisfaction, I have here abridged the largest Catechism, in such sort (I trust) as it may seem neither much defective in any necessary points of Christian Religion, neither very superfluous in any unnecessary circumstances, and amplifications, neither in consequence of matter greatly swerving from good order. That as the *least* Catechism is most meet for the first entering of children or others, though of more age, yet not of the greatest capacity; so might this of the *middle* sort serve, for such as having somewhat profited were yet desirous of further instruction; and lastly such, as not contented to know the chief points of Christian Religion briefly set forth, were desirous to see and understand the reasons and proofs of the same, may find in the *largest* Catechism wherewith to content and satisfy their minds; so that none should lack instructions of Godliness meet for them, of what age or capacity soever

---

[2] Nowell's Longer Catechism, 1570, (available at: https://archive.org/details/catechismwritten00noweuoft/page/106/mode/2up).

they were. The which three Catechisms being purely translated into the *Latin* tongue, may not only serve young beginners, or more forward Scholars in the Grammar School, to the same uses, and to the learning of true Religion, and the right use of the *Latin* speech, with one labor; but the last also might seem not unprofitable unto many Ecclesiastical Ministers for diverse good purposes.

Might it therefore please your good *Lordships* in respect of the former and other good considerations, which may unto your Wisdoms better appear, to allow the same, I shall think my little labor right well bestowed. And humbly taking my leave, I commend you unto the grace of Almighty God, Who have the same always in his blessed keeping.

November, 1572.

Your good Lordships to command,
A. N.

CHRISTIAN RELIGION

God's Word. Testament.

Master. Scholar.

Master. **Tell me, my Child, of what Religion thou art?**
Scholar. Of the same Religion which our Savior taught, whereof I am called and do trust that indeed I am a Christian.
Acts 11:16.

Ma. **What is the Christian Religion?**
Sch. Christian Religion is the true worshiping of God, and keeping of his Commandments.
Math. 4:10. John 4:24

Ma. **Of whom, or where is it to be learned?**
Sch. Out of the Word of GOD, which is written in the Books of the old and new Testament.
John 5:30. Acts 17:11. 2. Tim. 3:15-17.

Ma. **Why is God's word named the Testament?**
Sch. Because God's will, what he would have us to do, or flee, is there perfectly and unchangeably contained: from the which we out not to swerve on any side.
Gal. 3:15, 17. John 4:25. Gal. 1:8-9. Deut. 4:3. Isa. 3:11.

Ma. **By what means shall we come to the knowledge of God's will written in his Word?**
Sch. By diligent reading and studying of the same, or by hearing it read, and truly taught.
John 5:30. Acts 17:11.

Ma. **Is that sufficient?**
Sch. Because no man can by his own wit or diligence attain to the knowledge of God's wisdom, in his Word contained, we must with continual and fervent prayer crave of GOD, that it would please him by his holy Spirit, to endue our hearts with understanding and belief of his holy Word, and with earnest desire to obey his will therein declared.
1 Cor. 2:21; 3:7. Psalm 119:33-35. John 19:13.

Ma. **Which be the chiefest parts of the Word of God?**
Scho. The Law and the Gospel.
John 1:17. Luke 16:16. Acts 1:3, 30. Rom. 6:14-15.

Ma. **How be these two known, the one from the other?**
Sch. The Law teacheth us our duty towards God, and our Neighbor, and chargeth us straightly to do the same: promising everlasting life to such as do fulfill the Law, and threatening eternal damnation to such as do break the same.
Math. 22:37-40. Luke 10:27-28. Rom. 10:5. Gal. 3:10.

Ma. **What doth the Gospel?**
Sch. It promiseth that GOD, through faith in Christ, will be merciful to forgive the offenders of the Law, such as be sorry therefore, and purpose to amend.
Math. 2:15. Luke 5:32. John 1:17. Acts 3:38-39, & 15:38-39.

Ma. **How many parts be there of true Religion?**
Sch. There be two principal parts of Religion, likewise as of the Word of God; out of the which, as it were the spring head, Religion doth flow.
Rom. 1: 5:10, & 6:14-15.

Ma. **Which be they?**

Sch. Obedience, which the Law commandeth: and faith, or belief, which the Gospel requireth.

John 14: 14-15, 21. 23. . Rom. 10, 5:8. Mark 1:15. Rom. 1:5, 16. John 14:15, 21, 23-24. Mark 16:16. Acts 2:21. Rom. 19:12-13. John 14, 15:21, 23-24. Gal. 3:10.

Ma. **For more plainness, I would have thee to make more parts of Religion.**

Sch. I may (I think) conveniently reckon these four as chief parts of true Religion: Obedience, Faith, Prayer, and the Sacraments.

I. The Law:
The Ten Commandments

Master. **Well then: I will enquire of those four in order, as you have rehearsed them. And for that true obedience which is the first part, it is to be tried by the rule of God's Law; I think it necessary in beginning, to know what thou thinkest of God's Law.**

Scholar. I think the Law of God written in two Tables, to be the most perfect rule of righteousness, commanding all good things that are to be done, and forbidding the contrary.

Exo. 34:28-29. Psalm 19:6-10. Exod. 20. Deut. 5. Isa. 30:21. Mat. 22:36-37.

Ma. **Whereof treateth the first Table?**

Sch. Of godliness, or of our duty towards GOD; and it containeth the four first Commandments.

Ma. **The second, whereof treateth it?**

Sch. Of Charity, or love among men, and of our duties one towards another: which Table containeth six Commandments: and

so in the whole, the Law containeth ten Commandments.
Math. 19:18-19 & 22:39. Exod. 34:28. Deut. 4:13.

Ma. **Rehearse the first Commandment of the first Table.**
Sch. God spake thus: *Hear, O Israel, I am the Lord thy* GOD, *which have brought thee out of the Land of Egypt, out of the house of bondage. Thou shalt have no other Gods before me.*
Exod. 20:1-3. Deut. 5:5-7.

Ma. **Why doth he in the beginning tell us, that he is the Lord our God?**
Sch. In those words, his infinite Majesty, power, and goodness are expressed, whereby we are most straightly charged with obedience: unless we will be both rebels against him that is most mighty, and unthankful towards him that is most good and gracious.
Deut. 10:12-13. Malachi 1:5-6.

Ma. **What meaneth it, that he chargeth us to have none other Gods before him?**
Sch. He forbiddeth and condemneth all Idolatry.
Psalm 115:8-9. Math. 4:10.

Ma. **What is Idolatry?**

Sch. To reverence with Godly worship any creatures, or to put our trust or comfort in them as Gods; which to do, were most abominable. For we ought to give all Godly honor only to his Majesty, the greatest love to his goodness; to fly to him, and to crave his help in all fears and dangers: and with thankfulness to acknowledge that we owe ourselves, and all things that we have, unto his goodness.
Deut. 10:12-13, 20-21. Math. 22:37. Psalm 50:14-15, 23, 79:13, & 95:6-7, & 100:1-3. John 3:27. 1 Cor. 4:7. Jam. 1:17. Psalm 7:9 & 33:14.

Ma. **What mean those last words, Before me, or In my sight?**

Sch. That there is nothing so secret, that can be hid from him: and that therefore, not only with open life and outward show, but also with inward and pure godliness of the heart, we ought to honor him, and none but him only.
Isa. 29:13. Math. 5:8 & 15:8.

Ma. **Make me a brief rehearsal of such as thou dost think chiefly to break this Commandment.**

Sch. All Idolaters, as I have said, all Soothsayers, Conjurers, Sorcerers, Witches,

Charmers, and all that seek unto them : all false Prophets that do teach Lies : all that abuse the Word of GOD, or do not give the chief credit unto it, neither be guided by it, but do follow their own fantasy : all that fear, love, or esteem any creatures above GOD, or equally with him. All these and such like, do break the first Commandment of God.
Levit. 19:31. Eccle. 8:19 & 47:9. Deut. 18:20. Math. 15:2-3, 6, 9.

Ma. **Rehearse now the Second Commandment.**

Sch. Thou shalt not make to thy self any graven Image, nor the likeness of any thing that is in heaven above, or in earth beneath, or in the waters under the earth: thou shalt not bow down to them, nor worship them. For I the Lord thy God, am a jealous GOD, and visit the sins of the Fathers upon the Children, unto the third and fourth generation of them that hate me; **and** show mercy unto thousands in them that love me, and keep my Commandments.
Exo. 20:4, 23. Levit. 26:1. Deut. 4:15-19. Isa. 40:18, & 44:9.

Ma. **It may seem that this Law doth condemn the art of Painting and**

Graving; so that it is not lawful to have any images at all.

Sch. Not so: For in this first Table he speaketh not of any artificial thing civilly to be used, but only treateth of things which do appertain to the worshiping of God.
Math. 22:20, 21:36-37.

Ma. **What is then the meaning of this Commandment?**

Sch. In this second Commandment, God first forbiddeth us to make any Images to express or counterfeit him, or to seek him or to worship him in Images. And secondly, he chargeth us, not to worship the Images themselves or to abuse them in any wise by Idolatry or Superstition: but that we worship God alone in spirit and truth and as himself hath commanded us in his Word, to worship him, and not otherwise, after our own fantasies.
Isa. 40:18. Deut. 5:8-9. Psalm 97:7. Isa. 44-17.

Ma. **Why is it not lawful to express GOD with a bodily and visible form?**
Sch. Because there can be no likeness or agreeing between God, who is a spirit, eternal, infinite, unmeasurable, incomprehensible, and a bodily, frail, dead, and vain shape or Image.
Psalm 113:4-5, and 11:3-4. Isa. 40:18. John 4:24. Rom. 1:20, 23.

Ma. **What manner of worshiping is it which is here condemned?**
Sch. When we intending to pray turn ourselves to Images, fall down, and kneel before them, with uncovering our heads: or by other signs do show any honor unto them, as if God were presented unto us by them.
Lev. 25:1. Deut. 4:19, 5:9. Psalm 97:7, 115:8. Isa. 44:17. Acts 7:41.

Ma. **Rehearse the addition at the end of this Law.**
Sch. For (saith he) I the Lord thy God am a jealous God, and visit the sins of the Fathers upon the Children, unto the third and fourth generation of them that hate me.
Exo. 20:5. Deut. 5:9, 6:15. Psalm 78:58.

Ma. **Wherefore saith God these words?**

Sch. First, in naming himself *our Lord and our God*, he chargeth us to obey him in all things, both in respect of his authority and of his goodness, as was afore noted. And by the word *jealous*, he declareth that he can abide no partner or equal to be worshiped with him.
Deut. 10:12-13. 1 Kings 18:39. Malachi 1:5, 6. 1 Tim. 9:15, 19. Exo. 24:14. Isa. 42:8. Exo. 34:7. Isa. 14:20, 21.

Ma. **What is more said to forbid Idolatry?**

Sch. To restrain us from offending of him by Idolatry, which he so extremely hateth, he threateneth *that he will take vengeance, not only of them that shall offend, but also of their children and posterity*.

Ma. **Proceed thou in the text.**

Sch. As GOD by great threatenings scareth us from disobeying of him, so doth he with greater promises of his mercy and goodness assure us to obey him: promising that he will show great mercifulness, both towards all those that love him, and also towards thousands of their posterity.
Deut. 5:10. Exo. 34:6, 7.

Ma. **Where, before speaking of revenging, he nameth but three or four generations at the most: why doth he here speaking of mercy name thousands?**

Sch. To show that he is much more inclined to mercifulness, and to goodness, than to severity and sharpness.

Psalm 30:5, 103:8, & 145:8. Isa. 54:7-8, 10.

Ma. **Rehearse now the third Commandment.**

Sch. Thou shalt not take the Name of the Lord thy God in vain; for the Lord will not hold him guiltless that taketh his Name in vain.

Exo. 20:7. Levit. 19:12.

Ma. **Tell me what is it to take the Name of God in vain.**

Sch. To abuse it in blasphemy, sorcery, or witchcraft, in cursing, forswearing, or with swearing rashly, unadvisedly, or without necessity; or with once naming it without a weighty case and great reverence.

Isa. 8:19, & 52:5. Acts 19:13. 1 Tim. 1:10. Math. 3:33, 34. Psalm 113:1-2.

Ma. **Is there any lawful using of the Name of God in swearing?**

Sch. Yea forsooth, when an oath is taken for a just cause, either to affirm a truth, especially if the magistrate require or command it; or of any other matter of great importance, wherein we are either to maintain inviolate the honor of God, and to set forth his glory; or to preserve mutual agreement and charity among men. In these cases we may take an oath, using therein with great reverence the fearful and glorious Name of our God only, and of none other creature.
Exo. 22:11. Joshua 2:12. Psalm 15:5, & 63:12. 2 Cor. 1:23. Gal. 1:20. Heb. 6:26.

Ma. **What followeth next?**

Sch. For the Lord will not hold him guiltless, that taketh his name in vain.
Exod. 22:7. Levit. 19:10.

Ma. **Why doth he here particularly threaten them that abuse his Name?**

Sch. His meaning was, to show how highly he esteemeth the glory of his Name, to the end that seeing punishment ready for us,

we should so much the more heedfully beware of abusing it.
Levit. 19:12. Ezek. 20:9, 14.

Ma. **May we not then swear by the name of Saints, or by the name of other men, or creatures?**

Sch. No: For to swear, is nothing else but to call on him by whom we swear, to be a witness that we swear true: and to be a revenger of our lying, if we swear false. Which honor of knowing and punishing of all evil, being due to God's wisdom and Majesty only, to give to any other person or creatures, were a most heinous sin.
Exod. 22:11. Psalm 6:12. Heb. 6:16. Deut. 6:13. and 10:20. Joshua 23:7. Isa. 85:16.

Ma. **Rehearse the next Commandment.**

Sch. The fourth Commandment, which is the last of the first Table, is this: Remember that thou keep holy the Sabbath day. Six days shalt thou labor, and do all that thou hast to do: But the Seventh day is the Sabbath of the Lord thy God. In it thou shalt do no manner of work, thou and thy son, and thy daughter, thy man-servant, and thy maidservant, thy cattle and the stranger that is within thy gates. For in six

days the Lord made Heaven and Earth, the sea, and all that in them is, and rested the Seventh day. Wherefore the Lord blessed the Seventh day, and hallowed it.
Exo. 16:23, & 20:8-11, and 31:13. Levit. 23:3. Deut. 5:12-15. Ezek. 20:12. Gen. 2:1-3. Heb. 4:3, 9-10.

Ma. What meaneth this word, Sabbath?

Sch. Sabbath by interpretation signifieth rest. And that day (for that it is appointed only for the worshiping of GOD) the godly must lay aside all worldly business, that they may the more diligently intent to Religion and Godliness.
Exod. 16:23. Levit. 16:13. Jer. 27:21. Luke 23:56. Ezek. 46:3. Mark 6:2.

Ma. Why hath God set herein before us an example of Himself, for us to follow.

Sch. Because notable an noble examples do more thoroughly stir up and sharpen men's minds. For Servants do willingly follow their Masters, and Children their Parents. And nothing is more to be desired of men, than to frame themselves to the example and following of God.
Tobit 2:12. John 13:13, 15. 1 Cor. 4:15, 16, and 11:1. Eph. 5:1. 1 Pet. 2:21, 24.

Ma. **After what manner is the Sabbath day to be kept holy?**
Sch. The people must assemble together, to hear the doctrine of Christ, to yield confession of their faith, to make public prayers to God, to keep the memory of God's works, and to render thanks unto him for his benefits, and to celebrate the holy Sacraments which he hath left us.
Mark 6:2. Luke. 4:16. Act. 13:17. Math. 10:32. Psalm 95:2. Isa. 56:7. Math. 21:13. Eph. 5:21 1 Cor. 11:18, and 14:16.

Ma. **Is there no more required of us for the keeping holy of the Sabbath day?**
Sch. This is the outward rest and keeping holy of the Sabbath day; besides the which, there is a spiritual rest and sanctifying of it.

Ma. **What is that?**
Sch. That is, when resting from worldy business, and from our own works and studies, we yield ourselves wholly to God's governance, that he may do his works in us ; and when (as the Scripture termeth it) we crucify our flesh, we bridle the forward desires and motions of our heart, restraining our own nature, that we many obey the will of God, for thus doing, our

Sabbath day here upon earth, shall most aptly express a figure and likeness of eternal & most holy Rest, which we shall forever enjoy in Heaven.
Isa. 1:14, 16, & 58:13. Heb. 4:9-10. Gal. 5:14. Col. 3:5.

Ma. **Shall it be enough to have don those things every seventh day?**
Sch. These things indeed every man privately ought to record and think upon every day: But for our negligence and weakness sake, one certain special day is by public order appointed for this matter.
Psalm 1:2. & 84:4. Luke 18:1. Eph. 5:19.

Ma. **Hitherto thou hast rehearsed for me the laws of the first Table; wherein the true worshiping of God, which is the fountain of all good things, is briefly comprehended, and all evil things to God-ward be forbidden. Now therefore I would have thee tell me,**

What be the duties of our Charity and love towards men, which duties do spring and are drawn out of the same fountain, and which are contained in the second Table.

Sch. The second Table beginneth thus: Honor thy father and thy mother, that thy days may be long in the land which the Lord thy God giveth thee.
Exod. 20:12. Deut. 5:16. Math. 15:4.

Ma. **What is meant in this place, by this word, Honor?**

Sch. The honor of parents containeth love, fear, and reverence; and consisteth in obeying them, in serving, helping, and defending them; and also in feeding and relieving them, if ever they be in need.
Prov. 1:8. Mark 7:10-11. Coloss. 3:20. Heb. 12:9.

Ma. **Doth the law extend only to Parents by Nature?**

Sch. All that be in authority, or worthy of reverence, are meant by the name of Parents: as Princes, Magistrates, Ministers of the Church, Schoolmasters, Learned men, wise men, aged men, men of worship,

and such like.
Deut. 17:9-10. Rom. 13:1. Luke 10:16. Levit. 19:32. 1 Tim. 5:1. Prov. 5:13.

Ma. **Why are princes, magistrates, and other superiors, called by the name of Parents?**

Sch. To teach us that they are given us of GOD, both for our own and the public benefit; and so by the name of *Parents*, given to princes, magistrates, and other superiors, we are charged not only to obey them, but also to honor, and love them.
Rom. 13:4. Heb. 13:17.

Ma. **What followeth?**

Sch. That God will bless them who be obedient, and give due honor to their Parents, Princes, Magistrates, and other superiors, with long and happy life. And on the contrary part it followeth, that all such as do disobey or dishonor their Parents, Princes, Magistrates, or Superiors, shall come to a sudden, speedy, and shameful death: or else shall lead a life more wretched and vile than any death: and finally, for their disobedience and wickedness, shall suffer everlasting punishment in hell.
Exod. 20:12. Levit. 5:16. Eph. 6:23.

Ma. **Rehearse the sixth Commandment?**
Sch. Thou shalt not kill.
Exod. 20:13. Deut. 5:17.

Ma. **Shall we sufficiently fulfill this law, if we keep our hands clean from slaughter and blood?**
Sch. All things tending towards blood-shedding are also forbidden, as mocks, reproaches, quarrellings, fighting and such like.
Math. 5:21 & 19:18. James 2:11. Math. 5:21- 24. Rom. 3:13- 15. Gal. 5:20-21. James 3:14, 16.

Ma. **What more?**
Sch. God made this Law not only for our outward works, but also and chiefly for the affections of the heart. For, anger and hatred and every desire to kill, to revenge or to hurt, is before God adjudged manslaughter. Therefore these also God by his Law forbiddeth us.
Math. 5:22. Gal. 5:20-21 1 John 2:9-11.

Ma. **Shall we then fully satisfy the law, if we hate no man?**
Sch. God in condemning hatred, requireth love toward all men, even our enemies, yea so far as to wish health, safety, and all good

things to them that wish us evil, and do bear us a hateful and cruel mind : and as much as in us lieth to do them good, and to pray for them.
Luke 6:27-28. Rom. 12:14, 17, 19-20.

Ma. What is the seventh Commandment?

Sch. Thou shalt not commit adultery.
Exod. 20:14. Deut. 5:18. Math. 19:18. Prov. 6:14.

Ma. What dost thou think to be contained therein?

Sch. By this commandment is forbidden all kind of filthy lusts, all unchasteness of speech, all wantonness of countenance, and gesture, and all outward show of unchastity, whatsoever it be. Idleness likewise, excess of meat, drink, apparel, wanton plays, and pastimes and whatsoever else may occasion any uncleanness, either of body or mind, are forbidden by this commandment. For by this commandment, we are charged to keep our minds also clean from unchaste thoughts and desires, because as well our souls as our bodies, are the temples of the holy Ghost.
Math. 5:27- 29. Rom. 13:13. 1 Co. 6:9-10, 15-16, 18-19. 1 Thess. 4:3- 5, 7 &. 5:22. Ezek. 6:49, 56. Eccle. 33:26. 1 Cor. 3:16, 17, and 6:15, 19.

Ma. **Go on to the rest.**
Sch. The eighth commandment is: Thou shalt not steal.
Exod. 20:15. Math. 19:18.

Ma. **What is forbidden by this Commandment?**
Sch. Not only those thefts which are punished by man's law, are forbidden: but also we are charged that we deceive no man in buying or selling, by untrue and uneven measures or weights, or with deceitful or naughty wares: or by perverting of judgment with Bribes or gifts, or by any deceitful means. Further, all withdrawing of other men's duties, as withholding of the laborer's hire, refusing by covetousness to relieve the poor, to succor widows, fatherless children, and strangers, to leave the ignorant untaught, the simple uncounseled, the wandering and erring undirected, the sorrowful uncomforted, and such like, are by this law condemned.
Prov. 11:1, &. 20:10, 23. 2 Thess. 4:6. Titus 2:10. Psalm 62:10. Prov. 17:23. Isa. 5:23. Ezek. 22:13. Malachi 5:5. 1 Tim. 5:18. Prov. 14:20-21, 31. James 2:3, 6, and 5:19, 20. Levit. 19:9-10, & 23:22. Deut. 22:1-2, 34, and 24:15, 17, 19, & 27:17.

Ma. **Is any more contained in this Commandment?**

Sch. Yea forsooth. For all purpose and desire, to make our gain of others loss, is forbidden by this law. For that which is wrong before man to do, the same is evil before God once to will, or desire.
Zac. 8:16-17. Acts 20:33.

Ma. **What is the ninth Commandment?**

Sch. Thou shalt bear no false witness against thy neighbor.
Exod. 20:16. Deut. 5:20. Math. 19:18.

Ma. **What is the meaning of this Commandment?**

Sch. In this Law we are forbidden, not only open and manifest perjury, and breaking of our oath: But also all lying, slanders, backbitings, and evil speakings, whereby our Neighbor may lose his good name; and all flattery and dissembling whereby he may take harm. And that neither ourselves at any time speak any false or untrue thing; neither by words, writings, or silence, allow the same in other; but that we ever love, follow, maintain, and uphold the truth.

Exod. 23:1. Levit. 19:11. Deu. 19:18-19. Psalm 5:3. Soph. 3:18. Math. 19:18. Luke 3:14. 2 Pet. 2:12. Prov. 3:3, 12:19, & 23:23.

Ma. Is there any more meant by this law?

Sch. God who knoweth the secrets of our hearts, when he forbiddeth evil speaking, doth therewith also forbid wrongful misdeeming, and evil thinking of our Neighbors. Yea, and he chargeth us as far as truth may suffer, to think well of them: And to our uttermost power to preserve their good name.

Eccle. 37:15. 2 Cor. 13:28. Eph. 4:29. Math. 7:1. Rom. 14:4. 1 Cor. 13:5-7.

Ma. Now remaineth the last Commandment?

Sch. Thou shalt not cover thy Neighbor's house. Thou shalt not covet thy Neighbor's wife, nor his servant, nor his Maid, nor his Ox, nor his Ass, nor any thing that is his.

Exod. 20:17. Micah 2:1-2. Rom. 7:7, and 13:14. 1 Cor. 10:6.

Ma. **What is more commanded here than was before?**

Sch. God hath before forbidden evil doings & corrupt affectations of the mind; but now he requireth of us a more precise pureness, that we suffer not any desire, be it never so light, nor any thought, be it never so small, in any wise swerving from right, once to creep into our heart. For it is meet that even in our very hearts and minds, should shine before God most perfect pureness and cleanness. For no innocency and righteousness, but that which is most perfect, can please him: whereof he hath also set before us this Law as a most perfect Rule.
Psalm 19:16. Gal. 5:14. Jer. 4:13. Ezek. 18:3. Math. 5:18. Rom 12:2. Psalm. 5:4-5. 2 Cor. 6 :14.

Ma. **Now thou hast briefly told me the meaning of the ten Commandments, tell me: Cannot all these things that thou hast severally and specially declared, be in few words gathered as it were into one sum?**

Sch. Yes verily, seeing that Christ our heavenly schoolmaster hath comprised the whole pith and substance of the Law, in a

sum and short abridgment, in this manner, saying: Thou shalt love the Lord thy GOD; with all thy heart, with all thy soul, with all thy mind, and with all thy strength. And this is the greatest Commandment in the Law. And the second is like unto this: Thou shalt love thy neighbor as thy self; for in these two Commandments are contained the whole Law and the Prophets.
Math. 22:23. Mark 12:30. Luke 10:17.

Ma. What manner of love of God dost thou take here to be required?

Sch. Such as is meet for God: that is, that we acknowledge him, both for our most mighty Lord, and our most loving Father, and most merciful Savior. Wherefore to his love, is to be adjoined both reverence to his Majesty, and obedience to his will, and affiance in his goodness.
Deut. 5, 10:2, 17, 20. Psalm 25:1, 1:1, 31:1, 96:7-9. and 118:8.

Ma. What is meant by, All thy heart, All thy soul, and All thy strength?

Sch. Such fervency, and such unfeignedness of love, that there be no room for any thoughts, for any desires, for any meanings or doings, that disagree from the love

of GOD. For every godly man loveth God, not only more dearly than all his, but also more dearly than himself.
Deut. 6:17-18. and 30:6. Joshua 23:17. John 14:15, 21, 23-24. and 15:10. Math. 10:37-38. Luke. 14:26.

Ma. Now, what sayest thou of the love of our neighbor?

Sch. Christ's will was, that there should be most strict bonds of love amongst his Christians. And as we be by nature most inclined to the love of ourselves, so can there not be devised a plainer, nor shorter, nor more pithy, nor more indifferent a rule of brotherly love, than that which the Lord hath gathered out of our own Nature, and set before us : that is, that every man should bear to his neighbor the same good will, that he beareth to himself. Whereof it followeth, that we should not do anything to our neighbor, nor say nor think anything of him, which we would not have others to do to ourselves; or to say, or to think of ourselves.
John 13:34-35. 1 Cor. 13:45. Eph. 5:2, 29. Phil 2:1-3. 1 Thess. 4 :9-10. Math. 7:12, and 22:36. Luke 6:31. Rom. 13:8- 10. 1 Cor. 13:5-6.

Ma. **How far extendeth the name of Neighbor?**
Sch. The name of neighbor containeth not only those that dwell near us, or be of our kin, and alliance, or friends, or such as be knit to us in any civil bond of love; but also those whom we know not, yea and our enemies.
Math. 5:43-44. Luke 10:33, 36-37. 1 Thess. 4:9-10.

Ma. **Seeing then the Law doth show a perfect manner of worshiping God aright, and of unneighborly love, ought we not to love wholly according to the rule thereof?**
Sch. Yea certainly; and so much that God promiseth life to them that live according to the rule of the Law: and on the other side, threatneth death to them that break his Law, as is aforesaid.
Deut. 8:1, 11:22, 28 & 30:15, 17. Math. 19:17. John 2:50. Rom. 6:23, and 10:5.

Ma. **Dost thou then think them to be justified that do in all things obey the Law of God?**
Sch. Yea truly; if any were able to perform it, they should be justified by the Law: but we are all by original corruption of our

nature, of such blindness, wickedness, and frowardness that we can neither understand, nor are able or willing to do our duty required by the Law. And though there be someone found, that performeth some one or two outward points of the Law, yet doth he offend in diverse other: and the heart of man is ever swerving from the inward justice and innocency required by the Law. Wherefore none can be justified by the Law before God, for he pronounceth them all to be accursed and abominable, that do not fulfill all things that are contained in the Law.
Rom. 10:5. Gen. 6:5, and 8:21. Prov. 20:9. Rom. 7:14, 15. Gal. 2:16. Prov. 20:9. Deut. 27:36. Gal. 3:10. James. 2:10-11.

Ma. Doth then the Law set all men in this remediless estate?

Sch. The unbelieving and the ungodly the Law doth both set, and leave in such cause as I have spoken: who as they are not able to fulfill the least jot of the Law, so have they no affiance at all in God's mercy through Christ. But among the godly, the Law hath other uses.
Deut. 27:26. Rom. 3:10, and 8:7-8. Eph. 5:5-6. James 2:10.

Ma. **What uses?**

Sch. First, the Law, setting the perfect rule of righteousness before our eyes, stirreth up our diligence to direct our lives thereafter.
Deut. 6:6-7. Joshua 1:7-8. Psalm 1:2. & 19.

Ma. **What more?**

Sch. Secondly, when we perceive that the Law requireth things far above man's power, and do find ourselves too weak for so great a burden, the Law doth raise us up to crave strength at the Lord's hand.
Rom. 3:19 and 7:14-15. 2 Cor. 3:5. Psalm 119:12, 27-28, 33-34.

Ma. **Proceed.**

Sch. Further, when we behold in the Law, as it were in a glass, the spots and uncleanness of ourselves, it bridleth us that we trust not in our own innocency, and stayeth us for being proud in the sight of God.
Rom. 3:10-12, 19-20, & 7:7.

Ma. **Say on?**

Sch. When we find in our consciences, that we be guilty of sin, which is the breach of God's law, and do know also that by sin we do deserve the curse and most heavy wrath of God; and that the reward of sin is not

only all worldly misery, bodily diseases, and death, but also eternal damnation, and death everlasting: the Law showing us to be in this most damnable estate, striketh our hearts with fear, and with wholesome sorrow, and driveth us to repentance, and to seek pardon of our sins, righteousness, and life everlasting (which we cannot have by the Law), by and through Christ our Savior only.
Prov. 20:9. 1 John 3:4. Deut. 27:26. Gal. 3:10. Rom. 1:18, 2:8, 4:15, and 6:23. 2 Cor. 3:7, 9. Eph. 5:5-6. Rom. 3:20-22, and 5:15-16. Gal. 2:16.

Ma. **Then as far as I perceive, thou sayest that the Law is as it were, a certain Schoolmaster to Christ, to lead us the right way to him, by knowing of ourselves, and by repentance and faith.**

Sch. Yea forsooth: and withal, it right well appeareth, that the Law is not given in vain, though men be far unable to do their duty required in the Law.
Rom. 10:4. Gal. 3:10-12, 24. Rom. 3:33, 7:12-13, 16. Gal. 3:20.

II. The Gospel: The Apostles' Creed

Master. **Thou sayest true. Now my dear child, since thou hast, so much as it may be in a short abridgment, largely answered this matter of the Law and obedience: good order requireth that we speak next of the Gospel, which containeth the promises of mercy through Christ, to them that have broken God's Law, and be sorry therefore; to the which Gospel, faith hath especially respect. For this was the second point in our Division, and this also the very orderly course of those matters, that we have treated of, hath (as it were) by the hand brought us unto. Tell me therefore, what is the sum of the Gospel, and of our faith.**

Scholar. Even the same wherein the chief articles of our Christian Faith, have been in old time briefly knit up and contained, and which is commonly called the Creed, that is, our belief.

Ma. **Rehearse thy belief.**

Sch. I believe in God the Father Almighty, maker of heaven and earth. And in Jesus Christ his only Son our Lord. Which was conceived by the holy Ghost, born of the virgin Mary. Suffered under Ponce[3] Pilate, was crucified, dead, and buried. He descended into Hell. The third day he rose again from the dead. He ascended into Heaven, and sitteth at the right hand of GOD the Father Almighty. From thence shall he come to judge the quick and the dead. I believe in the holy Ghost. The holy Catholic Church. The Communion of Saints. The forgiveness of sins. The resurrection of the body. And the life everlasting. Amen.

Ma. **Into how many parts dost thou divide this whole Confession of faith?**

Sch. Into four principal parts. In the first whereof, is treated of GOD the Father, and the creation of all things. In the second, of

---

[3] Pontius

his Son Jesus Christ, which part containeth the whole sum of the Redemption of man. In the third, of the holy Ghost. In the fourth, of the Church, and of the benefits of God toward the Church.

Ma. **Go forward then to declare me these four parts in order: And first, in the very beginning of the Creed, what meanest thou by this word, Belief?**

Sch. I mean thereby that I have a true and a lively faith, that is to say, a Christian man's faith in God the Father, God the Son, and God the holy Ghost: and that I do, by this form of confession, testify and approve the same faith.

Math. 10:32, and 28:19. John 1:12-13. Rom. 1:17, and 10:9. Gal. 3:26. Heb. 4:14.

Ma. **Tell me as plainly as thou canst, What that same lively, true, and Christian faith is?**

Sch. Faith is an assured knowledge of the Fatherly good will of God toward us through Christ, and an affiance in the same goodness, as it is witnessed in the Gospel: which Faith hath coupled with it an

endeavor of Godly life, that is, to obey the will of God the Father.
John. 1:12-13. Rom. 8:1, 14, 38-39. Colos. 2:2-3. Heb. 10:22-23, and 11:1. Psalm 1:3. Math. 7:17-18, & 13:23. Gal. 5:6. 1 Pet. 1:13-15.

Ma. **Then thou hast learned, that no ungodly persons, which either despair of God's mercy, or fear not his justice, but lead a wicked life carelessly, can have the true Christian Faith, though they do rehearse the words thereof with their tongue.**

Sch. So I have learned indeed.

Ma. **Seeing there is but one God, tell me, Why in the confession of the Christian Faith, thou rehearsest three, the Father, the Son, and the holy Ghost.**

Sch. Those be not the names of sundry Gods, but of three distinct Persons in the Godhead. For God the Father, God the Son, and God the holy Ghost, being three persons, are one only God, as we are taught by the holy Scriptures; which we ought readily to believe, rather than curiously to search the infinite depth of so secret and hidden a mystery.

Math. 3:16-17, and 28:19. 1 John 5:7, and 14:7-11. 1 Cor. 8:5-6. Prov. 25:26.

Ma. **Thou sayest true. Go forward therefore, why callest thou God, Father?**

Sch. First and principally, for that the is the natural Father of his only son Jesus Christ. Secondly, for that he is our Father, both for that he created us, and gave life unto us all, and also for that he hath heavenly begotten us again through the holy Ghost; and by faith in his true and natural Son Jesus Christ, he hath elected, and adopted us his children; and through the same Christ hath given us his Kingdom, and the inheritance of everlasting life.

Psalm 2:7. Math. 3:17. John 1:14. Rom. 15:6. 2 Cor. 1:3. Gen. 1:27. Malachi 1:6, and 2:10. John 1:12, and 3:3, 5. Rom. 8:15- 17. Galat. 4:5-6. Eph. 1:5-6. Titus 3:7. 1 Pet. 1:3-5.

Ma. **Why dost thou name God, Almighty?**

Sch. For that he made all things and hath all things under his power, to order them after his will.

Isa. 40:21-22. Math. 5:45, and 10:29. Eph. 1:11. Heb. 1:23.

Ma. **Be wicked spirits and evil men also subject to God's power?**
Sch. Else could we never be out of fear, if they might have any power over us without the will of God. But we are upholden by this comfort, that neither Devils, nor wicked men can once stir, but at God's will or sufferance: and that we are so under the protection of our Almighty Father, that not so much as one hair of our head can fall to the ground, but by his will, who beareth us so good will.
John 1:10-12. Math. 8:31-32. Luke 22:31-32. John 10:28-29, and 19:10-11. Acts 2:.23-24, & 4:27-28, & 12 :11. Luke 21:18, and 22:7.

Ma. **Why is it added, that God is the Creator of heaven and earth?**
Sch. Because the greatness, wisdom, and goodness of God, which are of themselves incomprehensible, are to be seen in his works, as it were in a glass. For when we see that same unmeasurable greatness of the world, and all the parts thereof to be so framed, as they could not possibly in beauty be fairer nor for profit better; we forthwith thereby understand the infinite power, wisdom, and goodness of the Workman and Builder thereof.
Psalm 19:1, and 50:6. Rom. 2:19-20.

Ma. **How dost thou say that GOD created all things?**

Sch. That God the most good and mighty Father, at the beginning and of nothing, by the power of his Word, that is of Jesus Christ his Son, framed and made this whole visible world, and all things whatsoever they be that are contained therein, and also the incorporeal Spirits, whom we call Angels.

Gen 1:1. Psalm 33:6-7, & 89:11. John 3:1. Acts 14:15. 1 Cor. 8:6. Heb. 1:2. Coloss. 1:16.

Ma. **But dost thou think it godly, to affirm that GOD created all spirits, even those wicked spirits whom we call Devils?**

Sch. God did not create them such; but they by their own evilness fell from their first creation, without hope of recovery: and so are they become evil, not by creation and nature, but by corruption of nature.

Gen. 1:31. John. 8:44. Jude verse 6.

Ma. **Did God think it enough to have once created all things, and then to cast away all further care of all things from thence forth?**
Sch. No: but as God hath created all, so he upholdeth and governeth all: else would all soon run to utter ruin.
Psalm 75:3, 104:8-9, 145:14-15, and 147:5-6. Col. 1:16-17. Heb. 1:2-3.

Ma. **To what end dost thou think that Almighty GOD hath created and doth govern all things?**
Sch. The world itself was made for man, and all things that are therein were provided for the use and profit of man. And as God hath made all other things for man, so made he man himself for his glory.
Gen. 1:26, 29. Psalm 8:6-7, & 104:14-15. Proverbs 16:4. Isa. 43:7. Rom. 11:36. Coloss. 1:16.

Ma. **What hast thou then to say of the first beginning and creation of man?**
Sch. That which Moses wrote, that is: that GOD fashioned the first man of Clay, and breathed into him soul, and life: and afterwards out of the side of man, being cast in a sleep, he took out woman, and

brought her into the world to join her to man, for an helper and companion of his life.
Gen. 1:26, & 2:7, 18, 22-24.

Ma. **Whereat this day there is to be seen in both men and women so great corruption, wickedness, and perverseness: did God create them such from the beginning?**

Sch. Nothing less. For God being most perfectly good, can make nothing but good. God therefore at the first made man according to his own Image and likeness.
Gen. 1:26-27, 31. Coloss. 3:10.

Ma. **What was that Image, according to the which thou sayest that man was fashioned?**

Sch. It is most absolute righteousness, and most perfect holiness, which most properly belongeth to the very nature of God, the which Image was in man, until man by blots of sin marred the same.
Deut. 32:3-4. Rom. 9:14. Coloss. 3:10. 1 John. 1:5, 2:29, and 3:3. Wisdom of Solomon 1:13-14.

Ma. **Tell me how came this to pass.**
Sch. The woman deceived by the devil, persuaded the man to take of the fruit

which God hath forbidden them, whereby, the Image according to the which they were created, was defaced: and both they and their posterity became disobedient to God, froward and unable to all goodness ; and subject not only to all worldly miseries, bodily diseases, and temporal death, but also unto eternal death, and everlasting damnation.
Gen. 3:1. Wis. 1:13.14. 1 Cor. 2:14. Rom. 8:7-8. 2 Cor. 3:5. Rom. 6:23. Eph. 5:5-6.

Ma. But may it not seem that God did too rigorously punish the tasting of an Apple?

Sch. Let no man extenuate the most heinous offence of man as a small trespass, and weigh the deed by the Apple, and by the only excess of Gluttony. For he with his wife, catched and snared with the guileful allurements of Satan, by infidelity revolted from the truth of God to a lie: he gave credit to ye false suggestions of the Serpent, wherein he accused God of untruth, of envy, and of malicious withdrawing of some goodness. Having received so many benefits he became most unthankful towards God, the giver of them; he, the child of the earth, not contended that he was made according to the Image of God, with intolerable ambition and pride, sought to make himself equal with the Majesty of God: Finally, he withdrew himself from allegiance to his Creator, yea, and malepartly[4] shook off his yoke. Vain therefore it is to extenuate the sin of Adam. Gen. 3:3-6, 11, 22. Gen. 1:26-27. Psalm 8:4-6, and 104:14-15. Gen. 1:26-27. Coloss. 3:10. Hosea 6:7.

Ma. **But why should all the posterity for the Parents fault lose all the felicity, and fall to all misery?**

Sch. God endued Adam with those ornaments, to have them or lose them to him and his, that is to all mankind. And it could not otherwise be, but that as of an evil Tree, evil fruits do spring: so that Adam, being corrupted with sin, all the issue that came of him must also be corrupted with that original sin. Howbeit we need not so much to complain upon our Father Adam, seeing ourselves by our many and great sins are most deservedly fallen into all miseries, death and damnation: for delivery from which, there

---

[4] Archaic word meaning, an imprudent person.

remaineth no help or remedy in ourselves, or any other creature.
Math. 7:18, & 12:33. Rom. 5:12, 14, 17. Hosea 6 :7. Rom. 6:23. 2 Cor. 11:3. Eph. 5:6.

Ma. **What hope or comfort then is left, and in whom remaineth it?**

Sch. God promised that the seed of the woman, which is Jesus Christ the son of the virgin Mary, should bruise the head of the Serpent, that is of the Devil who deceived them; and so should deliver them and their posterity that believed the same. And this is it which now followeth in the second part of the Creed: I believe in Jesus Christ, etc.
Gen. 3:14, 15. Rom. 5:15, 16. Gal. 3:16, 19. Heb. 2:14-16.

Ma. **What signifeth this name, Jesus?**

Sch. Jesus in our tongue is, as much to say, as, the Savior. For Jesus Christ, the son of God and the son of the Virgin, hath delivered and saved us, which were held bound with wickedness and thrall in the foul bondage of the old Serpent the Devil, and were wrapped in the snares of eternal death.

Math. 1:21. Acts 10:38. Coloss. 1:13-14. Heb. 2:14-15. 1 John 3-8.

Ma. Who gave him the name of Jesus?

Sch. The Angel, by the commandment of God himself.

Math. 2:21. Luke 1:31, and 2:21.

Ma. Now tell me what meaneth this name of Christ?

Sch. It is as much to say, as Anointed: whereby is meant, that he by the holy Ghost is anointed the Sovereign King, Priest, and Prophet.

Psalm 2:6. Isa. 61:1. Dan 9:24-25. Luke 4:18. Acts 4:27. Acts 10:38. Heb. 1:9.

Ma. Is Christ's Kingdom a worldly Kingdom?

Sch. No, but a spiritual and eternal Kingdom, that is governed and ordered by the word and spirit of God, which bring with them righteousness and life.

Luke 1:32-33. John 18:36. Coloss. 1:13-14. 2 Tim. 4:1.

Ma. **What fruit take we of this Kingdom?**
Sch. It furnisheth us with strength and spiritual armor, to vanquish the flesh, the world, sin, and the Devil, the outrageous deadly enemies of our souls; and to live virtuously and holily.
Rom. 13:12, and 16:20. 2 Cor. 10:4.

Ma. **What manner of Priest is Christ?**
Sch. The greatest and an everlasting Priest, which only is able to appear before God, only able to make the sacrifice that God will allow and accept, and only able to appease the wrath of God.
Psalm 110 :4-5. Heb. 4:14-15, and 5:6-7, and 7:2-3, 11-12, and 9:13-14.

Ma. **To what commodity of ours doth He thus?**
Sch. For us he craveth and prayeth peace and pardon of God: for us he appeaseth the wrath of God : and us he reconcileth to his Father. For Christ alone is our mediator, by whom we are made at one with GOD. Yea, he maketh us as it were fellow Priests with him in his Priesthood, giving us also an entry to his Father, that we may with assuredness come into his

presence, and be bold by him to offer us and all ours to God the Father in sacrifice.
John 14:27. Acts 10:36. Coloss. 1:20. Heb. 9:14-15. 1 Tim. 2:5. Rom. 8:13, and 12:1. Gal. 4:5-6. Eph. 3:11. Heb. 4:15-16.

Ma. What manner of Prophet is Christ?

Sch. Whereas men despised all other Prophets and teachers, the servants of God; Christ himself the Son of God and Lord of all Prophets came down from Heaven, his Father's ambassador and messenger to men, fully to declare his Father's will, and to instruct men in the right knowledge of God, and of all truth. And so in the name of Christ are contained those three Offices which the Son of God received of his Father, and fulfilled, to make us partakers with him of all the fruit thereof. For the Son of God is not only called, and is indeed, Jesus Christ, that is, the Savior, King, Priest, and Prophet; but also he is so for us, and to our benefit and salvation.
Luke 7:16. Acts 7:37. Heb. 1:12. John. 8:26, and 15:15, 17:6, and 18:37.

Ma. **How dost thou call Christ the only Son of God, seeing also the godly are also named the children of God?**
Sch. For that Christ is the only natural Son of GOD: of one substance with the Father. And we being by nature the children of old Adam, are made the children of God by adoption, grace, and favor, through Christ our Savior.
Math. 2:15, and 3:17. John. 1:14, 34, and 14:10, 11. Heb. 1:2-3 and 5:5. Rom. 8:13-15. Gal. 4:4-5. Eph. 1:5. 1 John 3:1.

Ma. **What meaneth it that thou dost call Christ our Lord?**
Sch. For that the Father hath given him dominion over men, Angels and all things: and that he governeth the kingdom of GOD, both in heaven and in earth, with his own will and power.
Math. 9:6, and 10:1, 12, 18, and 28:18. Luke 1:32-33. Eph. 1:20-21.

Ma. **What more?**
Sch. Hereby are all the Godly put in mind, that they are not at their own liberty, but that both in their bodies and souls, and in their life and death, they are wholly subject to their Lord, to whom they ought to be

obedient, and serviceable in all things as most faithful servants.
Deut. 10:12, 20. Malachi 1:6. Luke 9:23-24, and 14:26-27. Heb. 2:5, 9-10.

Ma. **What followeth next?**
Sch. Next is declared, how he took upon him man's Nature, and hath performed all things needful to our salvation.

Ma. **Was it then necessary that the Son of God should be made Man?**
Sch. Yea: for necessarily it was, that what man had offended against GOD, man should abide and satisfy it: which most heavy burden, none but Jesus Christ both God and man was able to bear. Neither could there be any other mediator to make peace between God & man, but Jesus Christ both God and man.
Math. 1:17, 17:22-23, and 20:19. John 1:14, & 11:50-51. Rom. 5:5. 1 Cor. 15:21-22. Phil. 2:6-7. Heb. 2:9. 1 Tim. 2:5. Heb. 9:4-5, & 9:28. 1 Pet. 2:21, 24.

Ma. **What followeth?**
Sch. That, he was conceived of the holy Ghost, born of the virgin Mary.

Ma. **And why was he not begotten after the usual and natural manner?**
Sch. Because he who came to cleanse us from our sins, must needs be clean from sin himself. And therefore was most pure Lamb of GOD, Jesus Christ, by the marvelous working of the holy Ghost, conceived and born of the virgin Mary without sin.
John 1:19, 36. 1 Cor. 7:7-8. Heb. 4:15, and 9:14. Math. 1:23. Luke 1:31, 35.

Ma. **Why is the virgin Mary by name expressed?**
Sch. That Christ may be known to be that true seed of Abraham and David, of whom it was from God foretold, and foreshowed by the Prophesies of the Prophets: of which Abraham, David, and the Virgin Mary lineally descended.
Gen. 22:18. Isa. 11:1. Math. 1:1, and 22:42, Rom. 10:2.

Ma. **Proceed in rehearsing thy belief.**
Sch. He suffered under Ponce[5] Pilate, was crucified, dead, and buried.

---

[5] Pontius

Ma. **Why doth the Creed omit the story of his life, and passeth straight from his birth to his death.**
Sch. Because in the Creed are rehearsed only the chief points of our redemption, and such things as so properly belong to it, that they contain as it were the substance thereof.
Isa. 53. Acts 13:23, 27.

Ma. **Rehearse the order of his death somewhat more plainly.**
Sch. He was most wickedly betrayed by Judas his own Disciple. Who was with money corrupted, and hired thereunto: he was forsaken of all his disciples, denied and forsworn by Peter, falsely and maliciously accused by the Jews, condemned by Pilate the Roman President;[6] he was buffeted, scourged, crowned with thorns, and clothed in purple, and otherwise abused and scourged, both most cruelly and spitefully: and finally with his Cross laid upon his neck, he was hailed out of the City into the place named Calvary; where between two Thieves they villainously nailed him upon the Cross, upon the which

---
[6] Governor.

being extremely tormented, he suffered most painful and shameful death, sustaining withal torments of mind, more cruel than any bodily death.

Math. 26:14-15, and chapter 27. Mark 14:45, and chapter 15. Luke 22:47, and chapter 23. John chapters 18 and 19.

Ma. Did Christ suffer all this willingly, or unwillingly?

Sch. Notwithstanding that this most vile & cruel death was most terrible to his human nature, yet did he submit his will unto his Father's will, who had appointed him unto the same, and so he suffered the said vile reproaches, torments and most cruel death, both willingly obeying his Father, and most patiently praying for those who crucified him.

Math. 26:37-39, 41-42, 53, and 20:28. Mark 10:45. John 10:11, 15, 17, 18. Phil. 2:8. Luke 23:34.

Ma. Why would GOD have his most innocent Son to suffer such a shameful and painful death?

Sch. Christ became our surety & pledge unto his Father, to answer, pay, & suffer whatsoever we did owe, and had deserved. And therefore he (though himself most innocent) suffered for us most wicked sinners. And his Father laid our burden upon him, according to the rigor of the Law and Justice: that for his sake he might deal most mercifully with us.

Isa. 53. Rom. 1:3. 2 Cor. 5:31. Gal. 2:4. Eph. 1:3, 7. Coloss. 1:13-14, & 2:13-14. 1 Pet. 3:18, and 4:1. John 3:6. 2 Cor. 15:21.

Ma. **Rehearse me then the sum of those benefits which we enjoy by Christ's death.**

Sch. Christ, as I before touched, yielded himself in our stead and place, to satisfy for our sins before God his Father, to appease the wrath of God towards us for our disobedience, by the sweet sacrifice of his obedience, and to make us at one with God. And so Christ the most innocent Lamb of God was bound, to set us sinners at liberty who were in thrall unto Satan, death, and damnation. Christ most guiltless was accused and condemned by the sentence of a worldly Judge, that he might acquit us most guilty and most worthy to be condemned, before the heavenly judgment-seat. Christ by his precious blood shed for us, hath cleansed and washed away the spots and filth of our sins. And finally, Christ by his undeserved reproaches, most painful & shameful death, hath delivered us

from eternal pain, shame, and death everlasting, which we had most justly deserved by our sins, which sins are buried with Christ, and clean removed from the sight of God. And so all Christ's suffering is a medicine and remedy to all our miseries, whereunto we are fallen either originally by *Adam*, or afterwards by our own wickedness, so that we faithfully believe in him and embrace him.
Rom. 5:8, 10-11. 2 Cor. 5:18-21. Eph. 2:12-14, 17. Heb. 7:26-27, 9:12, 14, and 10:12, 14, 17. Rom. 8:1-2, 33-34. Col. 3:13-14, 20-21. Psalm 51:7. Heb. 9:14. 1 John 1:7. Rev. 1:5. 1 Pet. 2:21-22. Rom. 4:7-8. Coloss. 2:13-14. Heb. 10:17. Rom. 8:12.

Ma. **Notwithstanding, we do suffer death of the body, which is a parcel of the punishment due to sin.**

Sch. Death of the body which without Christ was the gate to Hell, is now by Christ made to all that believe in him the gate and passage into Heaven; even as he himself did by death enter into his Kingdom; so that death, which before was a punishment, is now by Christ become an advantage.
Luke 23:42. John 5:25-26. 1 Cor. 15:18, 21:54-55. 1 Thess. 4:13-14. Phil. 1:21-22. Rev. 14:13.

Ma. **Cometh there any other profit unto us by the death of Christ?**

Sch. Christ's sufferings and death is not only a medicine of our miseries, as I before noted, but also an example for us to follow. Eph. 52. 1 Pet. 2:21, and 4:1-2.

Ma. **Declare that more plainly.**

Sch. We ought after his example to be obedient unto the will of God our heavenly Father, & patiently to take all injuries at man's hands, and to crucify the wicked lusts of the flesh, and to be as dead and buried unto sin : so that we sin no more hereafter, after the example of Christ our Savior, who was crucified, dead, and buried for sin : and indeed naughty lusts (which otherwise are unbridled) are, in those who by faith do cleave unto Christ, by the virtue of his death, as it were crucified, and the burning heat of them so quenched by his blood, that they may easily be brought to obey the Spirit. So that we are helped by the virtue of his death, to perform that which we are moved unto by the example of his life and death.
John 13:15. Eph. 5:2. 1 Pet. 3:21, and 4:12. 1 John 2:6. Rom. 6:1, 4, 7, 11. Gal. 2:20, and 5:24. Coloss. 2:13. Gal. 2:20, & 5:14. Coloss. 2:13.

Ma. **Are we not hereby put in mind of our duty also towards Christ?**

Sch. We are indeed taught that we are not our own, to do what we wish ; but that we are wholly Christ's, who hath so dearly bought us, most bounden to obey him, and to do his will, most bounden to love him, who so dearly loved us first, being yet his enemies: most ready again to yield all that is ours, yea, and our selves wholly unto Christ, who hath given himself wholly unto us : most ready for his sake to forsake not only all worldly things and pleasures of this life, but also to lose our lives rather than we forsake Christ, and our love and duty toward him. For happy is the death that being due to nature, is chiefly yielded for Christ; for Him (I say), who offered and yielded himself to willing death for us, and who being the author of life, both will and is able to deliver us (being dead) from death; **and** to restore us to life everlasting. Rom. 14:7-8. 1 Cor. 6:20. 2 Cor. 5:15. 1 Thess. 5:10. Rom. 5:8, 10. Math. 10:37, and 16:25. Luke 9:23-24, and 14:46. Math. 16:25. Mark 8:35.

Ma. **Why dost thou also add, that he was buried?**

Sch. His dead body was laid in grave, that his death should be most evident, and that all men might certainly know it. For if he

by and by had revived, many would have brought his death in debate and question, and made it doubtful.
Math. 12:40, and 27:59-60. 1 Cor. 15:5.

Ma. What meaneth his descending into Hell?

Sch. That as Christ in his body descended into the bowels of the earth, so in his soul severed from his body, he descended into hell; and that therewith also, the virtue of his death so pierced through to the dead, and the very Hell itself, that both the souls of the unbelieving felt their most painful and just damnation for infidelity, and Satan himself, the Prince of hell, felt that all the power of his tyranny and darkness was weakened, vanquished, and fallen to ruin; and on the other side, the dead who while they lived, believed in Christ, understood that the work of their redemption was now finished, and perceived the effect and strength thereof with most sweet and assured comfort.
1 Pet. 1:19. John 8:24. 1 Cor. 15:54-55. Heb. 1:14-15. John 5:25, 28, 11:25, 26. Rom. 14:8-9. Coloss. 1:13-14, 19-20.

Ma. Now let us go forward to the rest.

Sch. The third day after he rose again, and by the space of forty days oftentimes showed himself alive, and was conversant among the Disciples, eating and drinking with them.
Math. 28:6, 9. John 20:14, 19, and 13:30-31. 1 Cor. 15:4-5.

Ma. Was it not enough that by his death we obtain deliverance from sin, and pardon?

Sch. That was not enough, if we consider either him or ourselves. For if he had not risen again, he could not be thought to be the Son of God, nor could he have been our Savior from death. But now rising from death to eternal life, he declareth the power of his Godhead, and hath shewed himself the Conqueror of sin and death, even of the Devil himself.
Rom. 1:4, & 6:4, 9-10, & 8:1-2. 1 Cor. 15:26, 54. Eph. 1:20. Phil. 2:9. Gal. 2:19-20.

Ma. What profit bringeth it to us, that Christ rose again?

Sch. Manifold and diverse. For from thence commeth unto us an endeavor, virtue, and strength, to live well and holily: thereby Christ endueth us with righteousness which before we lacked. And Christ by his

resurrection from death to life, is become to us the author of life, for from thence have we hope that our mortal bodies also shall one day be restored from death, and rise again, for that he hath made us partakers of his Resurrection and Life. For it cannot be, that Christ our Head rising again, should suffer us the members of his body to be consumed and utterly destroyed by death.
Rom. 4:25, and 5:15, and 6:4, 5:11-12. 1 Cor. 15:20. 1 Thess. 4:14. Coloss. 1:18. 2 Tim 2:21.

Ma. **Proceed.**
Sch. As the Scriptures do teach that Christ is risen for our Righteousness, so do they also teach, that we after his example should rise from the deadly works of sin, and live from henceforth into righteousness and holiness: for the performance whereof, Christ endueth us with strength, by the virtue and power of his glorious resurrection.
Rom 6:4, 9,-11. Eph. 5:23. Coloss. 3:12.

Ma. **What followeth in the Creed?**
Sch. He ascended into Heaven, and sitteth on the right hand of God the Father almighty.
Mark 16:19. Luke 24:5. Acts 1:9-10. John 12:8, 16:10, 28, and 20:17.

Ma. **Tell me how this is to be understood.**
Sch. Plainly that Christ in his body ascended into heaven, where he had not afore been in his body: and left the earth where afore he had been in his body.

Ma. **Is he then here in the earth no more with us?**
Sch. He did himself foreshow unto his Apostles that they should not have him always with them, which is to be understood of his bodily presence. In the nature of his Godhead, which filleth all things, he ever was in Heaven and with the same: and with his Spirit, he is always present in earth with his Church, and shall be present till the end of the world.
John 12:8, 17:5. Math. 18:20, and 28:20. John 14:18, and 16:7. Rom. 8:9.

Ma. **Then are we not left without his help and protection, though we have not his bodily presence?**
Sch. No, forsooth. For Christ sitting on the right hand of GOD, doth with his power, wisdom, and providence, rule and dispose the world, move, govern, and order all things: and as he promised, he sendeth

down his holy Spirit from heaven into our hearts, as a most sure pledge of his good will. By which Spirit he bringeth us from darkness and mist into open light, he giveth sight to the blindness of our minds, he chaseth sorrow out of our hearts, and doth comfort and strengthen us: and the same will he do unto the world's end.
Math. 28:18. John 16:7, and 17:1. Eph. 1:20, and 4:8. Phil. 3:9, 14. Coloss. 1:18. Rev. 11:15. Rom. 5:5, 9, and 8:4.

Ma. **Now as touching Christ, what dost thou chiefly consider, in his ascending and sitting at the right hand of his Father?**

Sch. It was meet that Christ which from the highest degree of honor and dignity had descended to the basest estate of a servant, and to the reproach of condemnation and shameful death: should on the other side, obtain most noble glory, and excellent estate, even the same which he had before, that his glory and majesty might in proportion answer to his baseness and shame.
Eph. 6:20. Phil. 2:8-9. John 17:5

Ma. **What profit take we of his ascending into heaven, and sitting on the right hand of his Father?**

First Christ, as he had descended to the earth, as into banishment for our sakes; so when he went up into heaven, his Father's inheritance, he entered in our name, making us a way and an entry thither, and opening us the gate of Heaven, which was before shut against us for sin. Moreover, he being present in the sight of God, as commending us unto him and making intercession for us, is the patron of our cause; who being our advocate, our matter cannot quail.
John 14:2-3. John 16:26. Rom. 8:34. Heb. 7:25, and 9:24. 1 John 2:1.

Ma. **But how can we follow his example in his ascending up to Heaven?**

Sch. We ought from henceforth to look up to Heaven, and to raise up our minds and hearts thither, where Christ is at the right hand of the Father; Bending all our thoughts and studies upon divine, eternal and heavenly things, and not upon earthly, worldly, and transitory things.
1 Cor. 15:47-48. Coloss. 3:1-2.

Ma. **What more?**
Sch. We are furthermore taught, purely and sincerely to worship Christ the Lord, now reigning in Heaven, not with any earthly worship, traditions, or vain inventions of men, but with heavenly and very spiritual worship, such as may best beseem both us that give it, and him who receiveth it.
Isa. 1:11, 16-17. Math. 5:8. John 4:20, 24.

Ma. **Now I would hear thee tell me shortly what thou hast learned of the last judgment, and of the end of the world.**
Sch. Christ shall come in the clouds of heaven, with most high glory, and with most honorable and reverend Majesty, waited on, and beset with the company and multitude of holy Angels. And at the horrible sound & dreadful blast of Trumpet, all the dead that have lived from the creation of the world to that day, shall rise gain with their souls and bodies whole and perfect, and shall appear before his throne to be judged, every one for himself to give account of their life, which shall be examined by the righteous and severe Judge according to truth.

Math. 24:29-31, and 25:31-32. 1 Cor. 15:52. 1 Thess. 4:16. 2 Pet. 3:10. Rom. 14:10, 12. 1 Cor. 4:4-5. 2 Cor. 5:10-11.

Ma. **Seeing death is certainly appointed for all men, how dost thou in the Creed say, that some shall then be Quick, or Alive?**

Sch. Saint Paul teacheth, that they which then shall remain alive, shall suddenly be changed, and made new, so that the corruption of their bodies being taken away, and mortality removed, they shall put on immortality. And this change shall be to them instead of a death, because the ending of corrupted nature shall be the beginning of a nature uncorrupted.
1. Cor. 15:51. 1 Thess. 4:17. 1 Cor. 15:53.

Ma. **Ought the godly in thinking upon this judgment, to be stricken and abashed with fear, and to dread it, and shrink from it?**

Sch. No, but rather to conceive great hope and comfort thereby. For he shall give the sentence, which was once by the Judge's sentence condemned for us: to the end that we coming under the grievous judgment of God, should not be condemned, but acquitted in Judgment.

Rom. 8:1, 13, 23, 38-39. 2 Cor. 1:7. Phil. 3:20. Titus 2:13. 2 Pet. 3:12.

Ma. **Since then thou hast now spoken of God the Father the Creator, and of his Son Jesus Christ the Savior, and so hast ended two parts of the Christian confession: now I would hear thee speak of the third part, what thou believest of the holy Ghost.**

Sch. I confess that the holy Ghost is the third person of the most holy Trinity, proceeding from the Father and the Son before all beginning, equal with them both, and of the very same substance, and together with them both to be honored and called upon.

Math. 28:19. 1 John 5:7, 10:22, 15:26, and 16:7. Acts 4:15-16, 5:3.

Ma. **Why is he called Holy?**

Sch. Not only for his own holiness: but also for that by him the elect of God and the members of Christ are made holy: for which cause, the holy Scriptures have called him *the Spirit of sanctification*.

Rom. 1:4, and 15:16. 2 Thess. 2:13. Titus 3:5. 1 Pet. 1:2.

Ma. **In what things dost thou think that this Sanctification consisteth?**

Sch. First we are by his divine inspiration newly begotten, and therefore Christ said that we must be born again of water and the Spirit. Also by his heavenly breathing on us, God the Father doth choose and adopt us to be his children, and therefore he is worthily called *the Spirit of adoption*, who is in our hearts as the Seal of our election, persuading and assuring us, that God's benefits through Christ are all ours.
John 3:5-6. Titus 3:5. Rom. 8:15, 23. Gala. 4:5-6. Rom. 8:14-15. 1 Cor. 1:22, and 5:5. Eph. 1:13-14.

Ma. **Proceed.**

Sch. The holy Ghost expoundeth and openeth the divine Mysteries unto our minds: and by his light the eyes of our Souls are made clear to understand them. By his judgement sins are either pardoned, or reserved. By his strength, sinful flesh is subdued and tamed, and corrupt desires are bridled and restrained. At his will, manifold gifts are distributed among the godly.
John 14:17, 20, and 16:13, and 20:22-23. 1 Cor. 2:10-11, 13, 15. Eph. 1:17. Rom. 8:5, 9. Acts 22:4, 17. 1 Cor. 12:4, 7.

Ma. **Hast thou any more to say hereof?**

Sch. In thy manifold and diverse discommodities, molestations, and miseries of this life, the holy Ghost, with his secret consolation, and with good hope, doth assuage, ease and comfort the griefs and mourning of the godly, which commonly are in this world most afflicted, and whose sorrows do pass all human consolation: whereof he had the true and proper name of *Paraclete*, or *the Comforter*. And finally by his power, our mortal bodies shall rise and be alive again. Briefly, whatsoever benefits are given us in Christ, all these we understand, feel and receive the works of the holy Ghost. Not unworthily therefore, we put confidence and trust in the author of so great gifts, and do worship and call upon him.
John 14:16, 26, 15:26, and 16:7. Rom. 8:11. 1 Cor. 12:4, 7, 12-13.

Ma. **Now remaineth the fourth part, of the holy Catholic Church: of the which I would hear what thou hast to say.**

Sch. I may briefly say, that the Church is the body of Christ.

1 Cor. 12:27. Eph. 1:22-23. Coloss. 1:18, 24.

Ma. **Yea, but I would have it somewhat more plainly and at large.**
Sch. The Church is the body of the Christian Commonwealth, that is the universal number and fellowship of all the Faithful, whom God through Christ hath before all beginning of time, appointed to everlasting life.
Rom. 12:5. 1 Cor. 12:12-13, 20:26. Eph. 1:4-5, & 30:9-10. Math. 25:34.

Ma. **Why is this point put into the Creed?**
Sch. Because if the Church were not, both Christ had died without cause, and all the things that have been hitherto spoken of, should be in vain and come to nothing.

Ma. **How so?**
Sch. Hitherto we have spoken of the causes of salvation, and have considered the foundations thereof, namely, how God by the deserving of Christ, loveth and dearly esteemeth us: how also by the work of the holy Ghost, we receive this grace of God, whereunto we are restored. But of these, this is the only effect, that there be a

Church, that is, a company of the godly upon whom these benefits of God may be bestowed.
Math. 16:18. Acts 20:28. 1 Cor. 12:13, 28. Eph. 3:9, 5:25, 7:3-5, 11, and 10:21. 2 Tim. 3:15.

Ma. Why dost thou call this Church holy?

Sch. That by this mark it may be discerned from the wicked company of the ungodly. For all those whom God hath chosen, he hath restored unto holiness of life and innocency.
Rom. 8:29-30. 1 Cor. 14:33. Eph. 1:4, 5:11-12.

Ma. Is this holiness which thou dost attribute to the Church, already in all points perfect?

Sch. Not yet; for so long as we live a mortal life in this world (such is the frailty of mankind) we are of very weak strength wholly to shun all kind of vices. Therefore the holiness of the Church is not yet fully and perfectly finisht, but yet very well begun. But when it shall be fully joined to Christ, from whom it hath all cleanness and pureness, then it shall be clothed with innocency & holiness, in all points fully and perfectly finished, as with a certain Snowy white and most pure garment.

Rom. 8:26. 1 Cor. 13:9. 2 Cor. 12:5, 9. 1 Cor. 13:10, and 15:52-53. Eph. 5:26-27. Rev. 19:8, and 21:2, 10, 11, 27.

Ma. **To what purpose dost thou call this Church Catholic?**

Sch. It is as much as if I called it *universal*. For this company or assembly of the godly is not pent up in a certain place or time, but it containeth the universal number of the Faithful that have lived, do live, and shall live in all places, and ages, since the beginning of the world: that there may be one body of the Church, as there is one Christ, the only head of that body.

Math. 28:19. Acts 2:5. 9:10. 1 Cor. 12:12. Eph. 1:21, 23, and 2:12, and 4:4-5.

Ma. **Now I would have thee tell, why after the holy Church thou immediately addest, that we believe the communion of Saints.**

Sch. Whereas GOD hath them that worship him purely and sincerely, in all Countries and places, and in all times and ages; all they, though severed in distant times and places, are yet members most nearly joined and knit together, of one and the self-same body, whereof Christ is the head. Such is the Communion that the godly have with

Christ, and among themselves. For they are most nearly knit together in community of spirit, of faith, of Sacraments, of Prayers, of forgiveness of sins, of eternal Felicity: and finally, of all the benefits that God giveth his Church through Christ. And they are joined together among themselves in sincere love, concord and unity. And because the communion of Saints cannot be perceived by our senses, nor by any natural kind of knowledge, or force of understanding, as other civil communities and fellowships of men may be; therefore it is here rightly placed among these things that are to be believed.
Coloss. 1:19. 1 Cor. 12:12, 16, 20, 2:19. Eph. 4:3-4, 15-16. Coloss. 1:18-19. Math. 13:34-35, 22:39. Rom. 12:5. 1 Cor. 10:24, 13:4-5. 2. Cor. 11:28-29. Gal. 6:2. Phil. 2:1-2.

Ma. **Is this Church which thou speakest of, a visible or invisible Church?**

Sch. Here in the Creed is properly entreated of the congregation of those, whom God by his secret election hath adopted to himself through Christ: which Church can neither be seen with eyes, nor can continually be known by signs. Yet there is a Church of God visible, or that may be

seen, the tokens and marks whereof he doth show and open unto us.
Rom. 8:30, 33, 39. Eph. 1:4,-5, 11. Coloss. 3:12.

Ma. **What be those tokens?**
Sch. Wheresoever the Gospel of Christ our Savior is sincerely taught, God by prayer truly called upon in the name of Christ, the holy Sacraments are rightly administered, the discipline duly used, there the company of Christian men and women assembled, is a visible Church of Christ.
Isa. 55:10-11. Luke 24:47. John 14:13-16, &. 16:23. Rom. 10:8-9. 1 Cor. 11:20-21, 23. Math. 18:16, 17:19-20, and 28:19.

Ma. **Are not then all they that be in this visible Church, of the number of the elect to everlasting life?**
Sch. Many by hypocrisy and counterfeiting of godliness, do join themselves to this fellowship which are nothing less than true members of the Church. But for as much as wheresoever the word of God is sincerely taught, and his Sacraments rightly ministered, there are ever some appointed to salvation by Christ: we count all the whole company to be the Church of God, seeing also that Christ promiseth, that

himself will be present with two or three that he gathered together in his Name.
Math. 13:19, 25, 47, 16:18-19, 18:17-20, 28:19. Isa. 55:10-11.

Ma. **Why dost thou after the Church make mention also of the forgiveness of sins?**

Sch. First, because the keys wherewith Heaven is to be opened & shut, that is, the power of binding and loosing, of reserving and forgiving of sins, which standeth in the ministry of the Word of God, is by Christ given and committed to the Church, and properly belongeth unto the Church. Secondarily, because no man obtaineth forgiveness of sins, that is not a true member of the Church which is the body of Christ: that is, such a one as doth not earnestly, godlily, holily, yea and continually, and to the end embrace and maintain the common fellowship of the Church.
John 20:22-23. 1 Tim. 3:15. Math. 24:13. John 15:45. Coloss. 2:18-19.

Ma. **Is there then no hope of Salvation out of the Church?**

Sch. Out of it can be nothing but damnation, death, and destruction. For

what hope of life can remain in the members when they are plucked asunder, and cut off from the head and body?
John 15:4-5. Coloss. 2:18-19. 1 Tim. 3:15.

Ma. **What meanest thou by this word, Forgiveness?**
Sch. That the faithful do obtain at God's hand pardon of their Offences. For God for Christ's sake, who hath satisfied or sin, freely forgiveth all that believe in him their sins: and delivereth them from judgement, damnation, and pain due for the same.
Psalm 32:1-2. John 3:16-17. Acts 23:38-39, and 26:18. Rom. 3:24-25, 28. Eph. 1:7. Coloss. 1:13-14.

Ma. **Cannot we then by godly works satisfy God, and by our selves merit pardon of our sins?**
Sch. Christ alone by the suffering of his pains, and with his death wherewith he hath paid and performed the penalty of our sins, hath satisfied God. Therefore by Christ alone we have access to the grace of God. We receiving this benefit of his free liberality and goodness, have nothing at all to offer, or render again to him by way of recompence.
Isa. 54:4-5. Rom. 5:8, 10. Gal. 2:16. Coloss. 1:20, 21. 2 Tim. 1:9-10. Heb. 9:14-15.

Ma. **Is there nothing at all to be done on our behalf, that we may obtain forgiveness of sins?**
Sch. The Lord promiseth that he will pardon sinners if they repent; if they amend, and turn their hearts from their naughty lives unto him. Wherefore repentance and amendment of life are necessary on our part, that we may obtain remission of our sins past.
Jere. 18:8. Ezek. 8:21, 30-32, and 33:14. Math. 4:17. Luke 5:32.

Ma. **How many parts be there of Repentance?**
Sch. First, we ought to acknowledge and confess our sins before God, and to be heartily sorry, and ashamed that we have offended his Majesty: and earnestly to hate and utterly to abhor sin. This sorrow some call *contrition*.
Psalm 32:3-5, and 51:3-4. Proverbs 28:13. Luke 15:18, 21. 1 John 1:8-9. Psalm 6:6-7, 28:3-4, 8, 17, 18, 31:9-10, and 51:17. 1.Cor. 11:31. 2 Cor. 7:9-11. Math. 27:3-4. 2 Cor. 2:6-8. Luke 7:38, 47, 15:18, 20-21, 18:13-14, 23:42-43, and 24:47. Acts 2:37-38, 3:19, and 16:30-31. 1 Tim. 1:15-16.

Ma. **What more?**
Sch. Lest the greatness of sorrow should bring us unto desperation, our minds are

comforted by Faith, which doth put us in good and certain hope of obtaining pardon of our sins at God's hand, through Christ our Savior. And this is that we profess, that *we believe the forgiveness of sins*.

Ma. Is man able in this fear, and these hard distresses, to deliver himself by his own strength.
Sch. Nothing less. For it is only God which strengtheneth man, despairing of his own estate, raiseth him in affliction, restoreth him being in utter misery, and by whole grace the sinner conceiveth this hope, mind, and will, that I speak of.
Psalm 23:3, 30:10, 51:7-8, 10-12, & 80:2-3, 7, 18. Acts 11:18. 2 Cor. 1:3-4. 2 Thess. 2:16, 27. 2 Tim. 1:25. Math. 22:30. John 11:25-26. 1 Cor. 15.

Ma. Now rehearse the rest of the Creed.
Sch. I believe the resurrection of the body, and life everlasting.

Ma. Because thou hast touched somewhat of this before, in speaking of the last judgement, I will ask thee but a few questions: whereto or why do we believe these things?

Sch. Although we believe that the souls of men are immortal and everlasting, yet if we should think, that our bodies should by death be utterly destroyed for ever, then must we needs be wholly discouraged, for that wanting the one part of our selves, we should never entirely possess perfection and immortality. We do therefore certainly believe, not only that our souls, when we depart out of this life, being delivered from the fellowship of our bodies, do by and by fly up pure and whole into Heaven to Christ, but also that our bodies shall at length he delivered from all corruption, restored to a better state of life, and joined again to their souls, being made glorious like to the body of Christ : and so we shall wholly be made perfectly & fully blessed, enjoying eternal life and endless felicity.
1 Cor. 15:14, 17-19. Luke 16:22, and 23:43. Rom. 8:11. 1 Cor. 15:42, 53. Phil. 3:21.

Ma. Then thou thinkest that the death of the body ought not to be feared of the godly.

Sch. Yeah forsooth. For we are thoroughly persuaded that death is not a destruction that endureth & consumeth all things, but a guide for us to heaven, that setteth us in

the way of a quiet ease, blessed and everlasting life.
Luke 23:43. John 11:25. Phil 1:21, 23. Rev. 14:13.

Ma. **Now thou hast declared the Creed, that is the sum of the Christian faith, tell me what profit we get of this faith?**
Sch. Righteousness before GOD, by which we are made heirs of eternal life.
Rom. 3:21-22. Gal. 2:16.

Ma. **Doth not then our own godliness towards God, and leading of our life honestly and holily among men, justify us before God?**
Sch. Of this we have said somewhat already, after the declaring of the Law, and in another place to this effect. If any man were able to live uprightly, according to the precise rule of the Law of God, he should worthily be counted justified by his good works. But seeing we are all most far from that perfection of life, yea and be so oppressed with conscience of our sins, we must take another course, and find another way, how God may receive us into favor, than by our own deservings.
Rom. 7:14-15, 8:3, and 11:6. Gal. 2:10, and 3:10.

Ma. **What way?**
Sch. We must fly to the mercy of God, whereby he freely embraceth us with love and good will in Christ, without any of our deservings or respect of works, both forgiving us our sings, and so giving us the righteousness of Christ by faith in him, that for the same Christ's righteousness he so accepteth us, as if it were our own. To God's mercy therefore through Christ we ought to impute all our justification.
Luke 18:11-14. Rom. 3:24, and 4:4, 16. Eph. 2:4-5. 2 Tim. 1:9. Titus 3:4-5.

Ma. **How do we know it to be thus?**
Sch. By the Gospel, which containeth the promises of GOD by Christ, to the which when we adjoin Faith, that is to say, an assured persuasion of mind, and steadfast confidence of God's good will, such as hath been set out in the whole Creed, we do as it were take state and possession of this Justification that I speak of.
Rom. 4:9, 11, 24, 16:20-21. Gal. 2:16, 20, and 3:11. Heb. 10:38.

Ma. **Dost thou not then say, that faith is the principal cause of this Justification, so as by the means of**

faith we are counted righteous before God?

Sch. No, for that were to set faith in the place of Christ. But the spring-head of this Justification is the mercy of God, which is conveyed to us by Christ, and is offered to us by the Gospel, and received of us by faith, as with a hand. And so faith is not the cause, but the instrument of Justification, for that it embraceth Christ, which is our justification, coupling us with so strict a bond to him, that it maketh us partakers of all his good things.

Eph. 1:4-6, 2:4. Titus 3:4-6. Mark 1:14-15. John 1:12. Rom. 3:22, and 4:16, 19. 1 Cor. 1:30. Heb. 9:14.

Ma. But can he that hath this faith, lack good works?

Sch. No, for by faith we receive Christ unto us. And he doth not only set us at liberty from sin and death, and make us at one with God, but also (with the divine inspiration and virtue of the holy Ghost) doth regenerate and newly form us, to the endeavor of innocency and holiness, which we call newness of life.

Rom. 6:4, 7:6, 8:1, 9-10. 2 Cor. 5:17. Eph. 1:15, and 4:23-24. Coloss. 3:9-10.

Ma. **Thou sayest then that justice, faith, and good works do naturally cleave together; and therefore ought no more to be severed than Christ the Author of them can be severed from himself.**
Sch. It is true.
Rom. 5:1-2. 1 Cor. 13:2. James 2:20. 1 Peter 1:19 and chapter 2. Psalm 1:3. Math. 7:17-18, and 12:33-35. Rom. 6:1-4. Gal. 5:6. Eph. 3:17. Coloss. 2:6-7. Titus 3:8.

Ma. **Then this doctrine of Faith doth not withdraw men's minds from godly works and duties.**
Sch. Nothing less. For good works do stand upon Faith as upon their root. So far therefore is faith from withdrawing our hearts from living uprightly, that contrariwise it doth most vehemently stir up to the endeavor of a godly life ; yea and so far that he is not truly faithful, that doth not also to his power both sun vices, and embrace virtues, for living always as one that looketh to give an account.

Ma. **Therefore tell me plainly how our works be acceptable to God, and what rewards be given to them.**

Sch. In good works two things are principally required. First, that we do those works that are prescribed by the law of God. Secondly, that they be done with the mind and faith which God requireth. For no doings or thoughts, enterprised or conceived without faith, can please God.
Deut. 4:1-2. and 5:31-32. Mark 7:6-9, and 10:17, 19. John 14:11-15, and 15:10. Rom. 9:31-32, and 14:23. Heb. 11:6.

Ma. **Then if we both do such good works, and with such good mind & faith as God requireth, why should we not be righteous by our good works?**

Sch. Righteousness that is to be allowed before God the Judge, ought to be thoroughly perfect, and in all points to agree with the rule of God's Law: But our works, even the best of them, do swerve far from God's Law and Justice, and are many ways to be blamed and condemned; **wherefore** we can in no wise be justified before God by our works.
Luke 13:11-12, 14. Rom. 3:20, and 4:2. Job 4:18-19, and 15:14-16, and 25:4-6. Isa. 60:6. Psalm 14:2. Gal. 2:16.

Ma. **Doth not this doctrine withdraw men's minds from the duties of godliness, and make them slacker and slower to good works: at least less cheerful and ready to godly endeavors?**

Sch. No: for we are taught by the holy Scriptures, that as our sins do dishonor GOD, so do our good works serve to the setting forth of his Glory. No dread of hell therefore, and of damnation: nor hope of heaven and all joys, ought to keep us from sin, or to move us to virtue, so much as the fear of dishonoring the Majesty of God, and the desire of his Glory; which ought above all things to be most precious unto us. For as it is the greatest horror and mischief of sin, that God and his holy Word are thereby dishonored, so doth the honor and excellency of virtue stand herein, that God is thereby glorified. Further, good works do profit our Neighbor, both by deed, and by good example: and they do, as certain testimonies, assure us of God's good will towards us, and of our love and kindness again to God-ward, by keeping his Commandments: and they be witnesses of

our Faith, and so consequently of our salvation. Wherefore we may not say, that good works are unprofitable, or done in vain, and without cause, if we obtain not Justification by them.
Math. 5:16. 1 Pet. 2:12. Rom. 2:14. 2 Tim. 6:1. Titus 1:5. 2 Pet. 2:1. Math. 5:16. 2 Pet. 2:12. Math. 12:33. John 14:21-25, and 15:10. Phil. 1:12. 1 Pet. 1:9-10.

Ma. **But how can our good works which thou sayest are unperfect, even the best of them, please GOD, whose Justice is perfectness itself?**
Sch. It is faith that procureth God's favor to our works, while it is assured that he will not deal with us after extremity of law, nor call our doings to exact account, neither will use the severity of his Justice in weighing of them: but pardoning all their unperfectness, will for Christ's sake and his deservings, account them for fully perfect.
Rom. 9:31-32. Gal. 5:6. Heb. 11:4, 6. Psalm 130:3, and 143:2.

Ma. **Whereas then God doth by faith both give us Justification, and by the same faith alloweth and accepteth our work; tell me, dost thou think that this Faith is a quality of nature, or the gift of God?**

Sch. Faith is the gift of God, and a singular and excellent gift. For God instructing us with his word, and lightening our minds with his holy Spirit, maketh us apt to learn and believe those things that otherwise would be far from entering into the capacity of our dull wits, and weak faith. These things the Apostles understanding, do pray the Lord to increase their faith.
Math. 16:17. Mark 9:23-24. Job 9:38-39. 1 Pet. 3:21. Luke 24:24, 27:45-46. Rom. 10:8, 14, 16-17. Coloss. 1:9. 2 Tim. 1:7. Luke 17:5.

III. Praying: The Lord's Prayer

Master. **Thou hast in good time made mention of Prayer. For, now thou hast ended the declaration of the Law of God, and of the Creed, that is to say, of our Christian confession of Faith; it followeth next to speak of Prayer and of Thanksgiving. In the declaring of Prayer therefore, what order shall we follow?**

Scholar. This order, Master, if it so please you: first to show who is to be prayed unto; secondly, with what assistance; thirdly, with what affection of heart; And fourthly, what is to be prayed for.

Ma. **First then tell me who (as thou thinkest) is to be called upon.**

Sch. Surely none but God alone.

Ma. **Why so?**

Sch. Because our health, life, defense, salvation, and all good things do remain in God's hand and power, it is meet that we

ask all needful things of him, and in all distresses fly unto his help.
Psalm 17:7, 28, 46, 78, 104, 107.

Ma. **Why may we not call upon Saints, and other holy persons, which are departed out of this life, or upon Angels?**

Sch. For that GOD himself requireth our invocation upon him only, as being the peculiar and proper worship belonging to his Majesty, which we may not give to any other.
Psalm 50:15, and 89:26. John 16:23-24. Isa. 48:11.

Ma. **What more?**

Sch. If we should in prayer call upon any other, saving God only, we should do it without the warrant of God's word, and consequently without faith, which resteth upon God's Word: And therefore so to do, were a sin against God, and no service to God.
Rom. 10:8, 14:16-17, 23. Heb. 11:6.

Ma. **Now followeth next to declare with what confidence we wretched mortal men, that are so many ways unworthy, ought to call upon the immortal and most glorious God?**
Sch. We do not proudly come before God with our prayer, as though we of our selves were worthy to be heard : but knowing our own unworthiness, we come in the name of Christ our mediator, by whose intercession we trust to have access to the Majesty of God, and to the obtaining of his favor.
Psalm 79:8-9. Dan. 9:18. John 18:13, and 16:23-24. Eph. 2:18. 1 Tim. 2:5. Heb. 4:14, 16, and 10:19, 21.

Ma. **By what means conceivest thou this trust, that thou speakest of?**
Sch. I do believe the promises of God, made to us by Christ in the holy Scriptures, that whatsoever we ask with faith of God the Father in Christ's Name, we shall obtain so far as is expedient for us.
Math. 21:21-22. Mark 11:22-24. John 14:13, and 15:23-24. Heb. 10:19, 22-23. James 1:6-7, and 4:3.

Ma. **Now tell me, with what affection of heart we must pray unto God.**
Sch. If we do feel in our minds the grief of our miseries, and sins, that do oppress us,

as we ought to do, it can not be but that we shall have great desire of deliverance from that grief, and so with most fervent affection, shall we make suit to God for his help, with all prayers and supplications.
Psalm 6, 30:15, 38, & 124. Rom. 7:18, 8:22-23, 27, & 12:12. 2 Cor. 3:4-5. Luke 18:1, 5, 7. Eph. 6:18. Coloss. 4:1. 1 Tim. 2:1.

Ma. Is it not then enough to pray with tongue and voice alone?

Sch. GOD hath promised, that he will be near to help them only that call upon him truely, that is with their heart, and that their prayers do please him: wherefore it is also necessary that we do know that language wherein we make our prayers, that our tongue and mind may go together.
Psalm 34:15, and 145:18-19. 1 Cor. 14:7, 11, 14-15.

Ma. Is it lawful to ask of God, whatsoever cometh in our mind to desire?

Sch. God forbid that we Christians should ask of GOD, in Christ's name, any thing contrary to the will of God and our Savior Christ, and so unmeet for God to grant, and hurtful for us to receive. Wherefore lest we should in prayer be carried rashly by our own affections, Christ himself hath

prescribed a Form and Rule, after the which our prayers ought wholly to be directed.
Math. 7:11, and 20:23. John 16:13, 24. James 4:2-3. John 5:14-15.

Ma. What Rule and Form is that?

Sch. Even the same form of Prayer, which the same heavenly Schoolmaster appointed to his Disciples, and by them to us all: wherein he hath touched in very few points all those things that are lawful to be asked of God, and proper for us to obtain : which Prayer is after the Author thereof called *The Lord's Prayer.* If therefore we will follow the heavenly teacher with his divine voice, saying before us, truly we shall never swerve from the right rule of praying.
Math. 6:9-10. Luke 11:3.

Ma. Rehearse me then the Lord's Prayer.

Sch. When we shall pray (**saith** the Lord), say thus: *Our Father which art in Heaven, hallowed be thy Name. Thy Kingdom come. Thy will be done in earth, as it is in heaven. Give us this day our daily bread. And forgive us our trespasses, as we forgive them that trespass against us. And lead us not into temptation: but deliver us*

from evil. For thine is the kingdom, & the power, and the glory, for ever, amen.
Math. 6:9. Luke 11:2.

Ma. **Dost thou think that we are bound ever so to render these very words, that it is not lawful in one word to vary from them.**

Sch. It is no doubt, but that we may use other words in praying, so that we swerve not from the meaning of this Prayer, and do pray to God with such affiance and affection, as I have before spoken of.
This is evident by the book of Psalms and other prayers contained in the holy Scriptures.

Ma. **How many parts hath the Lord's Prayer?**

Sch. It containeth six: or as some divide it, seven petitions, but in the whole there are but two parts. Whereof the first belongeth only to the Glory of God, and containeth the three former Petitions: the second, which containeth the three or four latter Petitions, belongeth properly to our commodity and profit.

Ma. **Why dost thou speak so directly unto God in thy prayer, saying, Our Father?**

Sch. For that, I speak not as to one absent, or deaf: but I call upon God our Father, and pray to him as to one that is present, being surely persuaded that he heareth me when I pray; For else in vain should I crave his help.
Psalm 33:13-14, and 34:15, 17-18, and 94:9-11, and 139:1-2, and 145:18-19.

Ma. **Let us somewhat diligently examine every word. Why dost thou call God Father?**

Sch. Since sure trust of obtaining is the foundation of right praying, as hath before been declared: it was God's will that we should call on him by the sweetest name of *Father*: that we might have boldness to go unto him and in hope of his help, even as children do use to deal with their Father: yea, and with far better hope than any Children can have of their natural Father, how much God our Heavenly

Father, in ability, goodness and readiness to help us exceedeth all earthly Fathers.
Math. 22:21-22. Mark 11:22-24. John 16:23-24. Heb. 10:19, 22-23. James 1:6-7. Rom. 8:15-16. Gal. 4:6. Math. 7:7, 11. Luke 12:9, 13.

Ma. What else doth the name of Father teach us?

Sch. That we come to prayer with that love, reverence, and obedience, which is due to the heavenly father from his children, and that we have such mind, as becometh the children of God.
Malachi 4:6. Math. 26:39, 42.

Ma. Why dost thou call GOD our Father in common, rather than severally as thine own Father?

Sch. Every godly man may, (I grant) lawfully call GOD his own; But such ought the dear love among Christians to be, that every one should have regard to the common profit of all: For which cause in all this Prayer, nothing is privately asked, but all the petitions are made in the common name of all.
Psalm 22:1, 3. Rom. 1:8. 1 Cor. 1:4. Rom. 12:4-5. & 10:16. 1 Cor. 10:23, 13:5, and 22:12, 21, 25-26.

Ma. **What more?**

Sch. The rich and great men are taught not to disdain men of poor and simple state, but to regard them as their Brethren, whom God accepteth to the honor of his Children. And again, the poor and silly persons, which are most despised in this world, may yet in the mean time relieve themselves with this comfort, that in Heaven they have all one most mighty and most loving Father.
Malachi 2:10. John 8:41. Eph. 4:5-6. James 2:1-3, 5. Deu. 10:17. Psalm 10:17-18, 68:5-6, and 146:6-8.

Ma. **Why dost thou say that GOD is in Heaven?**

Sch. For that I believe that God reigning in eternal and highest felicity, posesseth the power of Heaven, and therewith also holdeth the governance of all things, and is each-where present, seeth, heareth, and ruleth all things.
Psalm 12:4-5, 20:6, 33:13-14, 13:4-6, and 115:3.

Ma. **What more?**

Sch. We are withal admonished, not to ask any thing meet for God, but as speaking to our heavenly Father, to have our hearts raised from the earth, and despising earthly things, and thinking upon things above and

heavenly, continually to aspire to that most blessed felicity of our father, and to heaven, as our inheritance by our heavenly Father, through Christ our Savior.
Coloss. 3:1. Rom. 8:17. Eph. 1:14, 18. Heb. 9:15. 1 Pet. 1:3-4.

Ma. **This then so happy a beginning, and entry of Prayer being now opened unto us, go to, rehearse me the first Petition.**
Sch. First, we pray that *God's name be hallowed.*

Ma. **What meaneth that?**
Sch. Nothing else, but that the name of God be made known to mortal men, and that his praise and glory be every where magnified here in earth, as it is meet to be. And that the names of all feigned gods being utterly abolished, the only divine name and Majesty of God, the heavenly father be had in honor, and called upon with pure minds by men of all ages, Countries, and parts of the World.
Joshua 24:14, 23. Psalm 89:5-6. 96:1-3. 97:7, 9, and Psalms 113, 115, 135, and 145. John 4:23-24. Rom. 1:23, 11:36, and 16:27. 1 Cor. 10:31. Eph. 3:20-21. 1 Tim. 1:17.

Ma. **What more?**

Sch. We pray that the holy name of GOD be not evil spoken of, for our faults, and as it were dishonored thereby: but rather that his Glory be by our own godliness towards GOD, and goodness towards men, every where magnified.

Isa. 52:5-6. Ezek. 30:20-21. Rom. 2:24. Math. 5:16. 2 Thess. 2:11-12.

Ma. **Go forward.**

Sch. Secondly, we pray *that God's kingdom come,* that is, that he suffer not the divine truth of his word (and Gospel of Christ) whereby he reigneth in good and godly men's hearts, to lie hidden in darkness ; but that it daily more and more be made manifest and well known to all men, being instructed with the heavenly doctrine of the same. And that he would resist and overthrow the craft and violence of Satan, and wicked men, that labor to darken the truth with lies, or to oppress and root it out by cruelty.

Math. 9:38, 24:14, 28:19-20. Luke 4:18-19. Rom. 7:17, 20. 2 Cor. 3:15-16, and 4:2, 4. Eph. 6:18-19. 1 Thess. 3:1-2. Math. 13:25, 38-39, 15:2-6. Mark 7:3-4, 7-9. John 16:2-3. and 17:14-15.

Ma. **Say on.**

Sch. We pray that GOD by his holy Spirit would illuminate, and govern the hearts of all such as be of his Church, wherein he reigneth specially as in his Kingdom ; and that he would strengthen them with his aid and Power as his Soldiers, that they may earnestly fight against, and subdue the Devil, the World, and the lusts of the flesh, to the enlarging of his Kingdom here upon the earth. And that lastly, all his, and our enemies being utterly trodden down, GOD may gloriously reign and triumph over all, and we by Christ may finally, as his Children and Heirs, be made partakers of his everlasting Kingdom.
John 16:13. Eph. 3:21. Luke 22:31-32. Rom. 6:12 8:5, 9, and 16:20. Gal. 5:15-16. Eph. 6:10, 17, 18-19. 1 Pet. 5:29. Math. 25:34, 41, 46. Rom. 8:16-18. 1 Pet. 1:3-4. Titus 3:7.

Ma. **What followeth?**

Sch. That God's will be done. For it is the duty of children to frame their life according to the will of their fathers, and not contrarywise the parents to conform themselves to the will of their children.
Psalm 40:8. Mark 26:39. John 5:30, and 6:38. Eph. 6:1.

Ma. **Whereto dost thou add, that God's will may be done in Earth as it is in Heaven?**

Sch. Whereas the minds of earthly men, burning with lusts are commonly carried to desire and do those things that most displease God: we pray that he will with the moving of his holy Spirit, so change and fashion all the wills of us, all to the will of his Majesty: that we may will or wish nothing that his divine will misliketh.
Rom. 8:5, 7. Rom. 8:9, 11, 14-15, 25. 1 Cor. 2:12, and 3:16.

Ma. **Proceed.**

Sch. We pray also that whatsoever we perceive to betide us by his will, we may receive and suffer it, not only with contented, but also with gladsome hearts. And that after the examples of his Angels, those heavenly spirits, and of his excellent creatures the Sun, Moon, and Stars, set before our eyes in Heaven, for like example of obedience to God's will, we in earth may be in all things likewise serviceable, and obedient unto his Majesty; that as in

Heaven so in Earth, there be no rebellion nor repining against God's holy will.
Acts 21:14. 1 Pet. 3:17, and 4:12-13. Psalm 19:1-2, 91:11, 103:20, 104:4, 135:7, and 136:7-9. Heb. 1:6, 7:14. Rev. 7:11, 19:10, and 22:9.

Ma. **What more?**

Sch. Seeing that God hath in his holy Scriptures expressly declared his Will, which he hath plainly notified, by giving them the name of his Testament, or last Will: they that vary from the meaning of the Scriptures, surely do manifestly depart from the will of God.
Deut. 4:2, 5:32, and 28:14. Math. 7:21, 12:50, and 25:3. 2 Cor. 3:6, 12. Gal. 3:15, 17.

Ma. **Now thou hast well answered touching the first part of the Lord's Prayer, which part containeth these three points that belong only to the glory of God. I think it good for us to go forward to the second part, which properly concerneth things profitable for our selves.**

Sch. The first point of the second part is, *Give us this day our daily bread.*

Ma. **What dost thou mean by the name of bread?**
Sch. Not only those things that minister us food and apparel, but also all other things universally, that are needful to the maintaining and preserving of our life, and the leading of it in quietness without fear.
Psalm 104:15, 27, 105:9-11. 144:10-11, and 145:14-16.

Ma. **Is there any thing else, whereof this word bread doth admonish us?**
Sch. That we seek not and gather together curiously dainty things for Banqueting, or precious Apparel, or sumptuous Household stuff, for pleasure: but that we despising delicacies and excess, be contented and satisfied with little, temperate, and healthful diet, and with mean and necessary apparel.
Psalm 78:18, 29-30, and 106:14-15. Math. 6:25. Luke 16:19. 1 Cor. 10:6. 1 Tim 6:7-9. Heb. 13:5.

Ma. **How dost thou call bread thine, which thou prayest to be given thee of God?**
Sch. By God's gift it becometh ours, when he liberally giveth it us for our daily uses, though by right it be not due to us.
Math. 7:7-8. 1 Cor. 4:7. 1 Tim. 6:17. James 1:17.

Ma. **Is there any other cause why thou callest it thy Bread?**
Sch. By this word we are put in mind that we ought to get our living with our labor, or by other lawful means, and that being therewith contented, we do never by covetousness or fraud seek any thing of other men's.
Gen. 3:19. Eph. 4:18. 2 Thess. 3:8, 10-12.

Ma. **Seeing God biddeth us to get our living by our own labor, why dost thou ask bread of him?**
Sch. Because that in vain shall we waste all the course of our life in toil of body, and travail of mind, unless it please God to prosper our endeavors.
Psalm 127:1. 1 Cor. 3:7.

Ma. **Thinkest thou that rich men also, which have flowing plenty, and store of all things, must daily crave bread of God?**
Sch. In vain shall we have plenty of all things, unless God by his grace do make the use of them healthful to us for the maintenance of our life. For which cause, even after Supper, we pray to have the daily meat, which we have already received, to be

given us of God: that is to say, to be made lifeful & healthful to us.
Deut. 8:3. Psalm 34:9-10 and 78:29-30. Luke 1:5, 3:4, and 12:15. 1 Tim. 6:17. Rev. 3:17.

Ma. **Why be added these words Daily, and this Day?**
Sch. That we avoiding all careful covetousness, and doing diligently our duty, should daily crave of our most liberal Father that, which he is ready daily to give us.
Math. 6:25, 34. Luke 10:41. Phil. 4:6. 1 Tim. 6:9-10. 2 Pet. 5:7.

Ma. **Go forward to the rest.**
Sch. Now followeth the fifth Petition, wherein we pray our Father *to forgive us our trespasses*.

Ma. **Is this asking forgiveness necessary for all men?**
Sch. Yea, for so much as there liveth no mortal man that doth not oft slip in doing of his duty, and that doth not oft and grievously offend God. They therefore that do not confess that they have sinned, nor do crave pardon of their defaults, but with that Pharisee do glory in their innocency and righteousness, before God or rather against God: they exclude

themselves from the fellowship of the faithful, to whom this form of prayer is appointed for them to follow, and from the hope of forgiveness of sins, which only remaineth in the mercy and goodness of God through Christ: For this is that which Christ saith, That he came into this world not to call the righteous, but sinners, to repentance.
Psalm 14:1, 3, 3:1-3. Rom. 3:10-11, 23. John. 8:7. James 2:10-11. 1 John 1:8, 10. Luke 18:9, 11, 13-14. 2 Cor. 5:15, 18. 1 John 1:7, 9, and 2:1, 12. Math. 9:13. 1 Tim. 2:15.

Ma. **Why is there a contrition added?**

Sch. It is most reasonable that we should pray that God would so forgive us, *as we forgive them that trespass against us.* For unless others do find us ready to forgive them, and unless we in following the mercifulness of God our father do show our selves to be his children, he plainly warneth us to look for nothing else at his hand, but extreme severity and punishment. For according to the same rule of rigor, and after the same example, shall justice without mercy be done upon him, that can not find in his heart to show mercy to other.
Math. 5:7, 6:14-15, 7:1-2, and 18:28, 35. Luke 6:36-38. James 2:13.

Ma. **May it not seem then, that our forgiving of men should deserve pardon of God: or be as a certain recompense made unto God?**

Sch. Not so. For then should not God's forgiveness be freely given: neither had Christ alone upon the Cross fully paid the pains of our sin due to us, for the which no man else could, or can, make any recompense or amends unto God.
Rom. 3:24-25, and 11:5-6. Gal. 5:4.

Ma. **Now go forward to the sixth Petition, which some do make two Petitions.**

Sch. Therein we pray, that he *lead us not into temptation: but deliver us from evil.*

Ma. **Why so?**

Sch. As we before do ask forgiveness of sins past, so now we pray that we sin no more. For we by nature are so unwary to foresee, and so weak to resist the manifold Snares, temptations and enticements of the Devil, the World, and the concupiscence of the flesh, that we cannot but be overcome, unless God do assist us with his grace, and arm us with his strength : and therefore we fly by prayer unto the protection, of our

almighty most loving Father, that he will not suffer us to be overcome with any wicked temptation, but that he will deliver and save us from all evil.
Math. 12:43-45. John 5:14, and 8:11. 2 Pet. 2:21-22. Math. 10:16, and 26:41. Luke 22:31-32. 1 Cor. 1:27. 2 Cor. 11:3. Eph. 6:10-12. James 1:14, and 4:1. 1 Pet. 5:8-9. 1 John 2:15-16. Rom. 16:20. 2 Tim. 4:17-18.

Ma. **There remaineth yet the conclusion of the Lord's prayer?**
Sch. For thine is the Kingdom, and the power, and the glory, for ever. Amen.

Ma. **Why would Christ have this conclusion added?**
Sch. To make us understand that GOD'S power and goodness is infinitely great, that there is nothing which he either cannot, or will not give us praying for it and asking it rightly. Which also this word *Amen*, which is to say, *So be it*, being added in the end of the Prayer, doth confirm unto us.
Math. 7:10-11 and 21:22. John 16:23. 1 Cor. 1:9-10, 20, and 9:8. Eph. 3:20. 1 Tim. 6:16. James 1:6.

Ma. **Why is there in the latter end mention made of the glory of God?**
Sch. To teach us to conclude all our Prayers with praises of GOD: for that is the end

whereunto all that we desire to obtain in our Prayer, and all our thoughts, words, and works, and all things universally ought to be preferred and applied. For to this end he hath created us, and placed us in this World.
1 Cor. 10:31. Eph. 3:20-21. Phil. 1:11. 1 Tim. 1:17. Jude verse 25.

Ma. **Go forward.**

Sch. Moreover, to praise and magnify God's goodness, justice, wisdom, and power, and to give him thanks in our own name, and in the name of all mankind, is parcel of the worshiping of God, belonging as properly to his Majesty as prayer; wherewith if we do not rightly worship him, surely we shall not only be unworthy of his so many and so great benefits as unthankful persons, but also shall be most worthy of eternal punishments, as wicked offenders against God's majesty.
Psalm 15:23, 29:1-2, 34:1-3, 50:14, 92:1-2, and Psalms 95, 96, and 103. Rom. 15:6. 1 Thess. 1:2 and 5:18. 2 Thess. 1:3. Luke 17:17. John 5:44. Rom. 1:21, 25. 1 Pet. 4:11.

Ma. **Since we also receive benefits of men, shall it not be lawful to give them thanks?**

Sch. Whatsoever benefits men do to us, we ought to account them received from GOD, because he alone indeed doth give us them by the ministry of men, so that our thankfulness to men, redoundeth to the glory of God, the true and last end of all things.
1 Cor. 12:6, 11. 2 Cor. 9:8, 12.

IV. The Holy Sacraments

Master. **Now we have ended our treating of the law of God, of the Creed or Christian confession, and also of prayer and of thanksgiving. Shall we not lastly of all conveniently speak of the Sacraments?**

Scholar. Most conveniently Master, for they have always prayers and thanksgiving joined to them.
Math. 5:16. 1 Pet. 2:12 and 4:10-11.

Ma. **Tell me therefore, how many Sacraments hath Christ ordained in his Church?**

Sch. Two: Baptism and the Lord's Supper.
Math. 26:26, and 28:19. John 3:5. Acts 2:58. 1 Cor. 11:23. Titus 3:5.

Ma. **What meanest thou by this word, Sacrament?**

Sch. A Sacrament is an outward testifying of God's good will and bountifulness towards us through Christ, by a visible sign, representing an invisible and spiritual grace, by which the Promises of God touching the forgiveness of sins, and eternal Salvation given through Christ, are as it were sealed, and the truth of them is more certainly confirmed in our hearts.

Math. 3:11, 26-28. Mark 16:16. John 3:5. Acts 2:8. 1 Cor. 20:16 and 11:24. Gala. 3:26-27.

Ma. Of how many parts consisteth a Sacrament?

Sch. Of two parts: of the outward element or creature, being a visible sign, and of that invisible grace.

Math. 3:11. and 26:16. John 3:5. 1 Cor. 10:16. Math. 2:11-12, and 28:9. John 3:5. 1 Cor. 10:16. Acts 8:36-38.

Ma. What is the outward sign in Baptism?

Sch. Water, wherein the person baptized is dipped, or sprinkled with it, *in the name of the Father, the Son, and the holy Ghost.*

Ma. What is the secret and spiritual grace?

Sch. Forgiveness of sins and regeneration: both which we have by the death and resurrection of Christ; and thereof we have this Sacrament as a Seal and Pledge.

Mark. 1:4. Acts 2:38. and 23:16. Rom. 6:3. Gal. 3:26-27. 1 Pet. 3:21.

Ma. **Show me the effect of Baptism yet more plainly.**

Sch. Where by nature we are the children of wrath, and none of GOD'S Church or household, we are by baptism received into the Church, and assured, that we are now children of God, and joined and grafted into the body of Christ, and become his members, and do grow into one body with him.

Eph. 2.:3, 19-20. Titus. 3:3-5. Math. 28:19. Mark. 16:16. John 3:5. Rom. 6:3. 1 Cor. 12:13. 2 Pet. 3:21.

Ma. **What is required of persons to be baptized?**

Sch. Repentance and faith.

Mark. 1:4, 15, and 16:16. Acts. 2:38, 8:36-37, 16:31, 33-34, 19:4-5, 22:16. 1 Cor. 12:13. Rom. 6:3, and 13:12-14. Gal. 3:26-27. Eph. 4:20-21.

Ma. **Declare the meaning of these more largely.**

Sch. First we must truly repent us of our former life, and believe assuredly that we are cleansed from our sins by the blood of Christ, and so made acceptable to God, and that his spirit dwelleth in us. And then according to this belief and promise made in Baptism, we must endeavor our selves to mortify our flesh, and by our good life to show that we have put on Christ, and have his Spirit given us.

Ma. **Why then are Infants baptized, which by age cannot perform these things?**

Sch. Because they be of God's Church; and God's blessing and promise made to the Church by Christ (in whose Faith they are baptized) pertaineth unto them. Which, when they come of age, they must themselves learn, believe, and acknowledge, and endeavor in their lives to express the duty at their Baptism promised and professed.
Gen. 9:9, 17:7-8. Mark 10:14, 18. Rom. 3:3 and 4:21-22. Gal. 3:27. Eph. 14:20-21. Coloss. 2:14.

Ma. **What is the order of the Lord's Supper?**

Sch. The same which the Lord Christ did institute: *Who in the same night that he was betrayed took bread, and when he had given thanks, he brake it, and gave it to his Disciples, saying: Take, eat, this is my Body which is given for you. Do this in remembrance of me. Likewise after Supper he took the Cup, and when he had given thanks, he gave it to them, saying: Drink ye all of this, for this is my blood of the new Testament, which is shed for you and for many, for remission of*

sins. Do this as oft as ye shall drink it, in remembrance of me. This form and order we ought to hold, and truly to keep, and to celebrate devoutly till he come again.
Math. 26:26. Mark. 14:22. Luke 22:19. 1 Cor. 11:23.

Ma. To what use?

Sch. For a continual thankful remembrance of his death, and the benefits that we receive thereby; and that as in Baptism we are born again, so with the Lord's Supper we may be always fed, and sustained, to spiritual and everlasting life. And therefore it is enough to be once baptized, as to be once born: But as we need oft to be fed, so is the Lord's Supper oft to be received.
Luke 22:19. 1 Cor. 11:24, 26. John 6:27, 32, 35, 48, 55-56. 1 Cor. 10:16.

Ma. Which are the parts of this Sacrament?

Sch. The parts hereof, even as of baptism, are of two sorts; the one is earthly and sensible: the other is heavenly, and removed from all outward senses.

Ma. **What is the earthly and sensible part?**

Sch. Bread and Wine, both which matters the Lord hath expressly commanded all to receive.

Math. 26:16, 27. Mark. 14:22-23. Luke 22:19-20. 1 Cor. 11:33, 35.

Ma. **What is the heavenly part and matter removed from outward senses?**

Sch. The body and blood of Christ, which are given, taken, eaten, and drunken of the faithful, in the Lord's Supper; only after a heavenly and spiritual manner, but yet verily, and indeed. In so much, that as the bread nourisheth our bodies, so Christ's body hath most singular force spiritually by faith to feed our souls. And as with Wine men's hearts are cheered, and their strengths confirmed, so with his blood our souls are relieved and refreshed through faith : which is the mean whereby the body and blood of Christ are received in the Supper. For Christ as surely maketh them that believe in him, partakers of his body and blood, as they surely know that they have received the bread and wine with their mouths and stomachs. And it is also a

gauge of our Immortality, and a pledge of our Resurrection.
John 6:27, 35, 48, 63. 1 Cor. 10:16. Psalm 104:15. John 6:54.

Ma. Is then the bread and wine changed into the substance of the body and blood of Christ?

Sch. No; For that were to destroy the nature of a Sacrament, which must consist both of heavenly and earthly matter: and to make a doubt of the truth of Christ's body: and to give occasion of grudging unto ye minds of the receivers.
Math. 26:26-27. Mark. 14:22-23. Luke 22:19-20. 1 Cor. 11:23-28.

Ma. Was this Supper ordained of Christ to be offered as a sacrifice to God the Father, for remission of sins?

Sch. No: For when Christ died upon the Cross, he once fully made that only everlasting Sacrifice for our salvation for ever; and hath left nothing for us to do, but thankfully to take the use and benefit of that eternal Sacrifice, which we chiefly do in the Lord's Supper.
Heb. 7:26. 9:11, 25, 10:9-10, 12, 14:18. Luke 22:19. 1 Cor. 11:24-26. Heb. 23:15-16.

Ma. **What is our duty to do, that we may come rightly to the Lord's Supper?**
Sch. To examine our selves, whether we be the true members of Christ.
1 Cor. 11:28-29.

Ma. **By what tokens shall we know this?**
Sch. First, if we heartily repent us of our sins. Next, if we stay our selves and rest in a sure hope of God's mercy through Christ, with a thankful remembrance of our Redemption purchased by his death. Moreover, if we conceive an earnest mind, and determinate purpose to lead our life godly hereafter. Finally, seeing in the Lord's Supper is contained a token of friendship and love among men, if we bear brotherly love to our neighbors, that is to all men, without any evil or hatred.
Jeremiah 24:7, and 29:12-13. Joel 2:12-13, 15-16. Luke 22:19. 1 Cor. 11:24-26. Rom. 5:5, 8-9, and 8:4-5. 1 Tim 2:14-16. 1 Pet. 1:13-14, 21-22, & 4:1-2.

Ma. **Having sufficiently, as I think, examined thee concerning the chief points of Christian Religion; I would see now, how briefly and sufficiently thou canst rehearse the whole sum of all that hath hitherto been said.**

Sch. First the Law of GOD contained in the ten Commandments, setteth before my eyes, a perfect rule of godly life, which I am bound to obey upon pain of eternal damnation: wherefore by the same Law, I do know my sin, and the wrath of God against me for the same, and that everlasting Death by God's Justice is therefore due unto me: which breedeth in me a horrible fear of mind, and trouble of conscience, from the which it being impossible for me to be delivered by mine own wisdom, power, or virtue, or by any help or means of man, or Angel, I am taught by the Gospel, that Christ the Son of God, being made man without sin, hath by his death suffered the punishment due for my sins, pacified the wrath of GOD his Father towards me, and reconciled me unto his favor again, and made me partaker of his own Justice, and Heir with him of everlasting life; of all which benefits of Christ I am made partaker by faith in him. Which faith the holy Ghost, by the preaching of the Gospel, hath wrought in my heart: confirming the same also by his holy Sacraments, being visible and most sure tokens and pledges of God's goodness towards me, through Christ. The which Faith as a lively and fruitful Tree, should bring forth in the fruits of good works, holiness, and righteousness all the days of my life, to the honor of God, who hath bestowed so many benefits upon me: and to the profit & good example of my neighbors. For the increase of the which faith, and grace to please God, and for the accomplishing all these things, I being of my self most weak and unable thereunto, ought to make continual and most earnest suit by hearty prayer unto God the father, the giver of all good things, in the name of his son our savior Jesus Christ: yielding always unto him most hearty thanks for all his benefits.

Math. 22:39. John 13:34-35. 1 Cor. 10:17, and chapter 13. Deut. 4:1, 2:13. Psalm 9:4, 19:6-7, 11. Math. 19:16-17. Luke 10:25-28. Rom. 2:12-13, 3:19-20, 4:15. Gal. 3:10. 2 Cor. 2:7, and 7:9-10. Rom. 1:15-16. Acts 13:38-39. Heb. 2:4-5 and 9:9, 12, 14.

and 10:2-4, 8. Math. 2:20-21. John 1:14, 29. Isa. 53:4-6, 10-11. Rom. 3:24-25.

Ma. **I do see, my good child, that thou well understandest the sum of Christian godliness. Now it resteth, that thou so direct thy life by the rule of this godly knowledge, that though seem not to have learned these things in vain.**

Sch. I will do my diligence, with God's help, worshipful Master, and omit nothing, so much as I am able to do, that I may answer the name and profession of a true Christian. And also I will humbly with all prayers and desires, always crave of Almighty God, that he suffer not the seed of his Doctrine to perish in my heart, as sown in a dry and barren soil, but that he will with the divine dew of his heavenly grace so water, & make fruitful the dryness & barrenness of my heart, that I may bring forth plentiful fruits of godliness, to be bestowed and laid up in the barn and garner of the Kingdom of Heaven.

Ma. **Do** so my good child; and doubt not, but as thou hast by God's guiding first conceived this in mind and will, so shalt thou by his grace attain to an happy and blessed end, of this thy godly study and endeavor, to thy eternal salvation; and to the glory of God, to whom be all honor, and glory, world without end.

A Selection of Prayers for Students & Scholars

An admonition for the morning.

Awake thou that sleepest, and stand up from the dead, and Christ shall give thee light.

It is time that we should now awake out of sleep.

The night is passed, and the day is come nigh, let us therefore cast away the deeds of darkness, and let us put on the armor of light.

Let us walk honestly as in the day: and put we on the Lord Jesus Christ.

Let our light so shine before men, that they may see our good works, and glorify our Father which is in Heaven.

Wisdom is a noble thing, and never fadeth away: yea, it is easily seen of them that love it, and found of such as seek it.

It preventeth them that desire it, that it may show it self unto them.

Who so awaketh unto it betimes in the morning, shall have no travail, for he shall find it sitting ready at his doors.

Wisdom excelleth foolishness, as far as light excelleth darkness.

A Psalm for the morning.

Praise GOD, O ye children of his servants: praise ye the name of the Lord.

Bless ye the name of the Lord: from this time forth for ever more.

The name of God is highly to be praised: from the rising up of the Sun unto the going down of the same.

The day O Lord is thine, and the night is thine: thou hast prepared the light and the Sun.

We have laid us down and slept, and are risen up again: for thou O God hast sustained us.

O God thou art our Lord: early in the morning do we seek thee, and with our prayer come before thee.

We are thy servants O Lord: grant us understanding, that we may know thy testimonies.

Make us to know the way that we should walk in: for we lift up our souls unto thee.

Teach us to do the thing that pleaseth thee, for thou art our Lord, let thy good Spirit lead us forth in the way of life.

Cause us to hear of thy loving kindness betimes in the morning, for in thee is our trust.

Replenish us early in the Morning with thy mercy: and we shall cry for joy, and be glad all the days of our life.

For thou O Lord art the thing that we long for, thou art our hope, even from our youth.

Through thee we have been maintained ever since we were born: thou art he that took us out of our mother's womb: our praises shall be always of thee.

We will sing of thy power, and will praise thy loving kindness betimes in the Morning: for thou hast been ever our strength, our refuge, our defense, and our most merciful Lord.

Glory be to the Father, and to the Son, and to the holy Ghost.

As it was in the beginning, is now, and ever shall be, world without end. Amen.

A Prayer for the morning.

We yield unto thee our most hearty thanks, O heavenly Father, for that thou hast delivered us from all perils and dangers of the night, and brought us safe to the beginning of this day: we beseech thee that thou wilt in the same, and ever hereafter, receive us into thy defense and protection: and as thou hast removed the darkness of the night, restored the light of the Sun, and raised us from sleep, so thou wouldest vouchsafe also to remove from us the inward darkness of ignorance, to raise us from the sleep of sin, and to lighten our minds with the heavenly beams of thy most holy Spirit, and with the knowledge of thy dear Son our Savior Jesus Christ, the true light of the World: that we eschewing the works of darkness, may guide the steps of our lives after the light of thy holy Word, walking comely as the children of light, in holiness and righteousness, as in the day, and in thy sight: and in the end, we may come to that most blessed eternal Light which thou dost inhabit, the same thy Son our Savior Jesus Christ being our guide thereunto. To whom, with thee, and the holy Ghost, one God of most glorious

Majesty, be all honor and glory world without end, Amen.

A Morning Prayer for scholars.

We render unto thee most hearty thanks, O Father of lights, the giver of all good gifts, that it hath pleased thee to move the minds of our parents and friends to set us unto the School in these our tender years, most meet for the learning of all good things : most humbly beseeching thee not to suffer their good hope and our best time to perish through our untowardness, negligence, and slothfulness. And because our watching, diligence and study can profit us nothing without thy Grace, vouchsafe with thy heavenly beams so to lighten our minds and wits, and to endue us with such desire and love of good Learning, Wisdom & Virtue, with such docility to conceive, and memory to retain the same, that we in our childhood and youth being well instructed in all good letters and virtue, may grow to be learned and godly men, to the profitable service of the Common-wealth, and of the holy Church, and to the setting forth of thy glory. This we crave at thy hands, O heavenly Father, in the name of thy only Son our Savior Jesus Christ, beseeching thee for his sake to grant the same. Unto thee, with the same thy Son and the holy Ghost, one God immortal, indivisible, and only wise, be all honor and glory, for ever and ever. Amen.

Another Prayer for scholars.

Grant, O Lord God heavenly Father, that we by thy divine Grace, setting the example of thy dear Son & most blessed child Jesus Christ before our eyes, as the most clear, and most notable example of all other to be followed, may even in these days of our childhood and youth, apply our selves wholly to all good and godly learning, and to the obedience of thy most Holy Will ; and that as in and that as we shall grow in years, we may also increase more and more in good knowledge, wisdom, and virtue, and in the love of all godly men: and specially in thy heavenly grace and favor, wherein resteth perfect felicity, through the same our Savior Jesus Christ. To whom, with thee, and the holy Ghost, be all honor and glory, for ever and ever. Amen.

An admonition for the evening and night.

IF any man walk in the day, he stumbleth not, because he seeth the light of this world.

But if a man walk in the night, he stumbleth: because there is no light in him.

This is the condemnation, that light is come into the world, and men loved darkness rather than light, because their deeds were evil.

Jesus Christ the Son of GOD is the light that shineth in darkness: the true light which lighteneth every man, that cometh into the world.

Let us therefore walk, while we have light, lest the darkness come upon us: for he that walketh in the dark, looketh not whither he goeth.

Let us not bear a strange yoke with unbelievers, but while we have light, let us believe on the light, that we may be the children of the light.

Let us believe in Jesus Christ the Son of God, who came a light into the world, that whosoever believeth on him, should not abide in darkness.

Whosoever followeth Christ, the light of the world, he doth not walk in darkness, but shall have the light of Life.

There ariseth up light in the darkness unto them that deal uprightly.

He that saith, how that he is in the light, and yet hateth his Brother, is in darkness even until this time.

He that loveth his Brother abideth in the light, and there is no occasion of evil in him.

If thou hast compassion upon the hungry and freshest the troubled Soul: then shall the light spring out in the darkness, and the darkness shall be as the noon day.

The Psalms for the evening and night.

IT is a good thing to make confession and prayer unto GOD: and to sing Psalms and praises unto thy name, O thou most highest.

To set forth thy loving kindness early in the morning: and thy truth in the night season.

While darkness covereth the earth and thy people, let thy glory O Lord, shine upon us, and send forth thy light and thy truth to direct us.

O GOD, who commandeth the light to shine out of darkness, shine in our hearts, and give us the light of the knowledge of thy glory, in the face of Jesus Christ.

Lighten our candle, O God our Lord: and make our darkness to be light : that we may walk before thee in the land of the living.

Thy Word is a Candle unto our feet and a light unto our paths : it giveth light to them that sit in darkness, and in the shadow of death: it guideth our feet into the way of peace.

Direct our steps in thy Word, and so shall our feet be kept from falling, and no wickedness shall have dominion over us.

O Lord, with thee is the Fountain of light, lighten our eyes with the light of thy countenance, lest that we sleep in death, and our enemies prevail against us.

Bring us out of darkness, and out of the shadow of death. Break our bonds asunder, deliver our souls from death: O save us from that darkness, where is weeping and gnashing of teeth.

Open our eyes that we may be turned from darkness to light, and from the power of Satan unto thee our God.

That we may receive forgiveness of sins, and inheritance among them which are sanctified by faith, that is, toward thy Son Jesus Christ.

So shall we lay us down in peace, and take our rest; for thou O GOD only makest us to dwell in safety.

Glory be to the Father, and to the Son, and to the holy Ghost.

As it was in the beginning, is now, and ever shall be, world without end. Amen.

A Prayer for the evening and night.

O Lord God in whose defense the safety of mankind, and all things, doth rest : now the light hath darkened the world, and our bodies shall be laid asleep (than the which nothing is more like unto death) we betake our selves wholly unto thy protection : most humbly beseeching thee that thou wilt deliver us from the power of wicked spirits, the Princes of darkness, which to deceive us can transform themselves into Angels of light ; and from all sin, the works of darkness, and from all other perils and dangers both bodily and ghostly, and that thou suffer us not wholly to be oppressed, and as it were buried in sleep, neither our minds so to be darkened that we forget thee, but that whilst our bodies are asleep, our hearts may continually wake and watch unto thee. And when that rest hath refreshed our bodies and minds sufficiently, as much as is requisite to nature, the next morning may make us more able and ready to serve thee, in the state of Life, wherein thou hast placed us, to the health of our own souls, the benefit of our neighbors, and the glory of thy holy

Name, through our Savior Jesus Christ. To whom with thee and the holy Ghost, be all honor and glory now and for ever. Amen.

Another Prayer for evening and night.

Almighty GOD, who as thou hast made the day for labor and travel, so hast thou created the night for the rest and refreshing of our wearied bodies and minds : we most humbly beseech thee, that as the night darkeneth and shadoweth all things, so thou wouldest for thy dear Son Jesus Christ's sake, hide our sins, removing them from thy sight, and putting away the memory of them by eternal oblivion, that as our bodies shall have the rest of sleep, so all our minds by hope of thy mercy, may enjoy the rest of a quiet conscience: and so being wholly refreshed, we may awake and rise unto thy service the next day, and all the days of our life: and when death itself shall come (from the which it is as easy for the to raise us, as from bodily sleep) we may rest in hope of that most joyful resurrection, wherein our bodies shall awake unto that everlasting day, which shall never be interrupted with any darkness : when we shall be made partakers of the inheritance of the Saints in light, in that most blessed City, the heavenly *Jerusalem*: where shall be no need of candle, neither of the Sun, nor of the Moon to lighten it : for thy glory O GOD, shall lighten it : and the Sun of the Lamb shall be our eternal light. Unto the which most glorious light, and kingdom of thy dear Son we beseech thee bring us, for the same our Savior Jesus Christ's sake: Unto whom with thee, and the holy Ghost, be all honor and glory, now and forever. Amen.

Finis.

Printed in Dunstable, United Kingdom